STILL MORE ON COACHING ARCHERY

STILL MORE ON COACHING ARCHERY

by **Steve Ruis**

Editor of Archery Focus Magazine

Library of Congress Cataloging-in Publication Data

Still More on Coaching Archery / Steve Ruis.
   p. cm
   ISBN 978-0-9913326-3-2 (softcover)
   1. Archery. 2. Coaching. I Steve Ruis, 1946-

ISBN: 978-0-9913326-3-2

The web addresses cited in this text were current as of December 2014, unless otherwise noted.

Writer: Steve Ruis; **Copy Editor**; Steve Ruis; **Proofreader:** Michèle Hansen; **Graphic Artist:** Steve Ruis; **Cover Designer**: Steve Ruis; **Photographers** (cover and interior): Steve Ruis and Claudia Stevenson unless otherwise noted; **Illustrator** Steve Ruis

Printed in the United States of America 10 9 8 7 6 5 4 3 2 1

Watching Arrows Fly
3712 North Broadway, #285
Chicago, IL 60613
800.671.1140

Dedication

This book is dedicated to all of my students who often help me understand things I did not and to my coaches who continue to humor me.

Steve Ruis
Winter 2014

Contents

General Commentary

Introduction

This book is, in essence, a continuation of **More on Coaching Archery** and **Even More on Coaching Archery** (hence the title). The contents are suitable for most coaches of archery and cover a wide variety of topics as the Table of Contents shows. It stems from the writing I do for *Archery Focus* magazine but well over half of the contents of this book have never been published anywhere before and so is entirely new.

I hope that the chapters herein stimulate discussion between coaches about how we go about our business and if you wish to write about your thoughts on any of these topics I extend to you an open invitation to do so, even if you want to write a "Ruis is crazy" article. Your work will be published in *Archery Focus* magazine to further the dialogue. In addition, I have established a coaching blog (*A Blog for Archery Coaches*) which is free and, when I last checked, had views from over 100 countries around the world and is up to almost 100 views per day. If you want to write a guest post for that blog, please send it to me at steve@archeryfocus.com and I will work with you to get it posted.

As before I write to you as both an archer and as a coach (more of one in some essays and more of the other in others). Also, as before, I do not assume that you will read this book in order, cover to cover, so there is some repition.

In most of the chapters I include references, mostly to *Archery Focus* magazine that you might find helpful regarding the topics of the chapters. *Archery Focus* magazine, founded by Rick McKinney and Yoshi Komatsu of Japan and continued by Claudia Stevenson and me is the largest trove of archery information in the world, so why not use it? A subscription to that magazine not only gives you the next six issues in the form of downloadable and printable PDF files, but access to all of the back issues, including thousands of articles, at no additional cost. The PDF formatted issues can be read on tablets and smart phones, too.

As to how many more of these books I can produce I forsee no more than two more as I have run out of cutsey titles (I still have Yet More . . . and Way More . . . in the wings.).

Your friend in archery,

Steve Ruis
Chicago, IL
Winter 2014
steve@archeryfocus.com

On Form and Execution

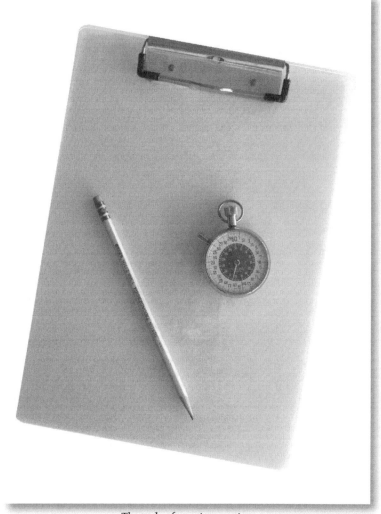

The tools of a serious copier.

Chapter 1
A Defense of Copying

We are all genetically primed to copy others, to "ape" their behavior as it were. Think about it: how do children learn from adults before they have even basic language skills? Through imitation, copying.

Is learning this way a good idea for archers? If you have read much of what I have written, you probably know I have decried the lack of a firm foundation upon which to base standard form and execution for archery. I have used phrases like "copycatting" and "monkey see, monkey do" as forms of disapproval for such practice. I have reconsidered my position on imitation, as I realized that what I am actually decrying is "doing it wrong." The problems I see are not in copying, they are in not copying correctly.

In a Broader Context

If one takes a bit of a step back and just looks at the 1970s you will see that compound form was a bit, well, . . . uh, odd looking to archers of today (*see photo*). According to my

sources, a great many compound archers shot this way: leaning back, hunched bow shoulder, crooked neck, etc. Is anyone shooting this way today? The answer is clearly "no." And the reason is the top archers discovered more effective techniques and others "copied" them.

When the Olympics re-incorporated archery in 1972, you could see some quite unusual things going on. One Japanese archer was drawing with her bow over her head as was done traditionally in Japan (I lost the photo). Again, is anyone doing this today? No. You can see champions with idiosyncratic form (Michele Frangilli comes to mind), but you don't see many people copying them.

The reason for this is there is an uncontested middle ground. The variations in form and execution in the very best archers is hard to see therefore people tend to conform to the "middle ground." They tend not to copy highly idiosyncratic champions because most people don't want to stand out as being "different" unless their performance is superior, in which case standing out is okay (instead of just being "odd").

So, over the long run, copying has resulted in a great deal of conformity, and since it was focused on successful archers, this conformity is very close to optimal form. In other words, the general practice of copying has created a larger cadre of good archers than there was in the past.

Is What's True in General, True in Specific?

So, since copying the form and execution of champions has lead us to overall better form, is this a good idea for individuals?

Here's the problem: who is copying whom? Many archers have a favorite archer, someone they look up to. Currently at or near the top of my list is Jaime van Natta. Does this mean I should copy her form and execution? Uh, probably not. There all kinds of considerations that go into picking somebody to copy. Here is a list of things I think are important:

- style
- height
- age
- gender
- injury history
- equipment
- mental makeup
- . . . there are more . . .

For example, if I want to become a professional archer, I would probably want to emulate a professional archer who has been successful in not only the sport of archery, but the business of earning a living in archery.

Obviously if the archer you really like shoots a compound bow and you shoot a longbow, there isn't much to copy. While that is maybe a ridiculous example, other style clashes might be between Olympic Recurve and Recurve Barebow or Compound Barebow and Bowhunter. Part of the benefit a youngling gets when imprinting on an adult (think of a duck and ducklings or a bear and her cubs) is the mental image of "this is the way a mature duck/bear/archer looks and acts." Ideally the younglings want to place themselves into that picture, so the more the person being copied looks and acts like you do, the better, as it will be easier to see yourself in them. So, ducks shouldn't imprint on your family's dog; they aren't going to learn the nuances of being a duck from Fido.

You want to "copy" someone of about the same age, the same gender, someone who shoots the same style, and has the same mental makeup. If you are easy going, you don't want to copy the actions of a hot head. If you shoot at a relatively slow tempo, do you want to imprint on "Machine Gun Kelly" over there?

If You Are Going to Copy Someone, Go For It

Most people who say they are using "Archer X" as a model, aren't. At most they are "wishing and hoping" that they could learn to shoot as well as Archer X does and it ends about there.

If you really would like to copy someone, you have to study them, in their native habitat as it were . . . on the shooting line. So, you will need a notebook, something to write with, binoculars (to see better) and a stopwatch. The first order of business is to write down their shot sequence, and I am not saying "stand, nock, draw, . . ." because if you want to see how their shot works you need details. What kind of stance do they have (open, closed, square, oblique, "special")? How wide is their stance? Do they move their feet during an end? How much care do they exercise when taking their stance? Is there anything unusual about their stance? The same kind of "research" needs to go into all of the other form elements in their shot sequence.

After you look at the parts of your model's shot, then you need to see how it is put together. This is where the stopwatch comes into play. To get a general time for the shot as a whole, I time from the raising of the bow to the release of the string. A great many timings need to be taken to see how consistent his shots are. In addition, during long ends (5 or 6 arrows) is there a break between shots (like six arrows being shot as two groups of three with a rest in between) or are the shots taken in a consistent rhythm throughout?

All of these things can be compared to "standard form" which is that described in "How to Shoot" books. By doing this you may discover the reasons for certain departures from standard form. For example, a great many experienced compound archers do not do a full followthrough. After the shot is away, the bow is pulled back toward the archer and dropped into a more comfortable position. This is done to lessen the wear and tear of holding such a heavy bow at arm's length. Should you copy this? No! Only after tens of thousands of shots can you tell a really good shot from one that isn't without the information the full followthrough gives you. This is something you earn through experience, not something you learn by copying.

And If All Else Fails . . .

If all else fails, walk up to your idol and ask them questions.

Really?

Really. They aren't demigods. Most are what I would call really nice people. Of course, you want to be respectful as you would be to anyone else you had a high opinion of. Do ask if they have the time then and there to answer a couple of questions, don't just blurt them out. (They might be getting into "competition mode" and not want to be distracted at the moment.) Yes, it is okay to ask for their autograph. Most of these folks are really quite friendly and always willing to help archers on the way up – well, pleasant respectful archers anyway.

Conclusion

Copying the form and execution of an archer who is roughly your body shape, shoots your style, and has roughly the same temperament is not a bad thing. Doing it lackadaisically is. Doing it half-heartedly is. Without actually making a significant effort, to say you are copying someone is just another form of magical thinking, but thinking that has no real magic.

Additional Learning References

So, You Want to Emulate a Pro by Tom Dorigatti (AFM, Vol 14, No 4) also in **ProActive Archery** by Tom Dorigatti (Watching Arrows Fly, 2012), Chapter 37, "Emulating a Pro ProActively"

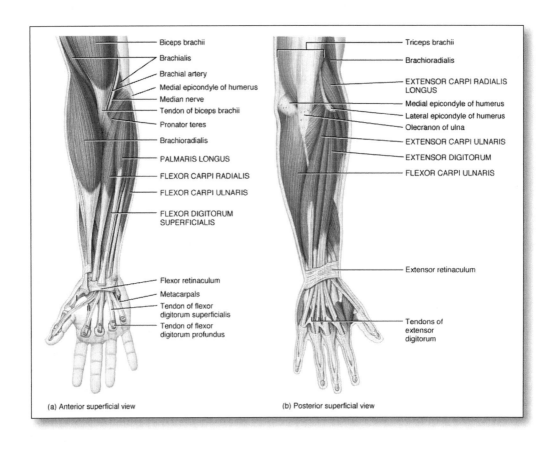

Biceps brachii
Brachialis
Brachial artery
Medial epicondyle of humerus
Median nerve
Tendon of biceps brachii
Pronator teres
Brachioradialis
PALMARIS LONGUS
FLEXOR CARPI RADIALIS
FLEXOR CARPI ULNARIS
FLEXOR DIGITORUM SUPERFICIALIS

Flexor retinaculum
Metacarpals
Tendon of flexor digitorum superficialis
Tendon of flexor digitorum profundus

(a) Anterior superficial view

Triceps brachii
Brachioradialis
EXTENSOR CARPI RADIALIS LONGUS
Medial epicondyle of humerus
Lateral epicondyle of humerus
Olecranon of ulna
EXTENSOR CARPI ULNARIS
EXTENSOR DIGITORUM
FLEXOR CARPI ULNARIS

Extensor retinaculum

Tendons of extensor digitorum

(b) Posterior superficial view

Chapter 2
An Analysis of the
New NTS Finger Loose

A recent graduate of a USA Archery Level 4-NTS training course noted that the current NTS teaching regarding releasing the finger grip on the string is to "relax the fingertips only." Since this is almost anatomically impossible it drew my attention. What the heck are they saying? Is this a translation problem? Here is my analysis.

Your fingers are controlled by muscles in the upper forearm. If you place your relaxed string hand, back down on a table top, it looks a little like a dead spider as the fingers are curled in their relaxed state. If you slowly engage the flexors controlling your fingers, your fingers curl up making a loose "fist." If you closely watch this happen each whole finger curls simultaneously. This is because the tendons serving these fingers do not perfectly separate the motions on each phalange. You cannot move just the fingertip on a finger and not move the rest. (You might also note that moving one finger tends to move another. If you use your pinky to experiment with—the finger you have the least control over—you will notice that moving that finger also moves the ring finger. This is because they share tendons to some extent.)

If you relax the flexors, your hand will resume it's "dead spider" pose. If you now engage your extensor muscles, your hand will flatten out on the counter top. These muscles are also in the upper forearm and, like the flexors, only contract, but their tendons are attached on the other sides of the fingers (and are also shared to some extent).

To make a "hard" finger hook (or an American-style "deep hook") requires both sets of muscles. Starting from your relaxed hand on the table top, curl your fingers using the flexor muscles, then flatten the back of your hand using the extensor muscles and voilà—a hard hook. In other words you need to flex both sets of muscles to make a hard hook, at least without a bowstring being pulled. My thinking is that when the draw tension gets elevated, the extensors can be relaxed as the string hand is pulled, stretched, into the correct shape (back of the hand being roughly flat), so only the flexors are needed to maintain the hook.

One more point is that is that the flexors are much stronger that the extensors. We all have really strong grips, but if you make a fist with one hand and then wrap your other hand around it, you will have no trouble at all preventing yourself from opening the fingers on that fist. Your weaker hand's flexors can easily dominate your stronger hand's extensors.

So, the NTS is suggesting . . . what?

The phrase "relax the finger tips only" is almost an anatomical impossibility and, if one could do this magically somehow, the string would either not leave the fingers or you would get the sloppiest release ever made. In the NTS finger hook, the finger tips point back toward the archer. If they were relaxed, they could at best move to be inline with the second phalanges, which are at right angles to the string. Even if the string managed to slip off of one finger tip, it is still in a groove of the middle finger, the position of which is linked to the position of the middle phalange which is not relaxed.

Our brains are not wired to do impossible things, so what is an athlete to do to effect this? What are they likely to try? If you give muddy instructions, you don't get crisp results. But maybe there is some subtle psychological aspect involved.

So, is NTS recommending just that we relax the flexors as been the process all along?

This is the only thing that approximates the instruction to "relax the finger tips only" that makes any sense. Clearly opening the fingers actively is incorrect (too slow to get a clean release) but is this new instruction a situation in which a pre-set level of muscle tension in those extensor muscles is established and then simply held during the release? This is not a new action, just maintenance of an old one, so it is not the equivalent of the "opening the fingers to release the string."

One can see after having made our experimental hard hook above that if we relax the extensor muscles that the fingers move in toward the palm, which would be toward the string and could impede its leaving if the response were fast enough, which I do not think it is. So, that does not seem to be an issue.

Another major question I have at this point is whether any effects of doing this (whatever it is) are real or not. The big factor is time. Let's use a fairly large estimate of the time it takes the arrow to leave the string of 20 milliseconds (0.020 s) over a power stroke of roughly 18-20 inches. The arrow is accelerating from 0 mph to roughly 200 fps (~135 mph) in that time and across that distance. How many milliseconds does it take for the string to leave the fingers, over a distance of about one inch? I would guess that it would probably take no more than about 2-3 of those 20 milliseconds. During that time the flexors relax, the string pushes the (whole) fingers out of the way and supposedly the relaxed back of the hand stays roughly flat and prevents, to some degree, the fingers pressing on the string more than is desirable. And as the stronger flexors relax, the string moves forward and toward the archer, which is away from any influence that the weaker extensors relaxing would create. So, I think we can dismiss the role of the extensors in this event.

I am still unclear what the instruction "relax the fingertips only" means. Does this actually make a better loose of the string? How would you confirm that it does? The only way I know to address these questions would be to set up a electromyograph (measures nerve impulses sent to muscles), isolate the two sets of muscles and see if you can tell the difference between the looses that keep the extensors flexed and those that do not. Then you have to see if the results are different in the two cases, and if they are, which one is better. Has this been done? If so, I would like to see the paper. (Possibly one might also be able to use high-speed video but that seems problematic to me.)

This experiment would also tell us whether an expert does this automatically when loosing the string, as how many could have been trained in this "new technique" at this point? Is ordinary training all that is needed to create this or is additional training needed?

Still More on Coaching Archery

How does an archer learn to "just relax the fingertips?"

The last question I have is: if this can be taught, how do you train an athlete to do it? Setting up electromyographic sensors to give an athlete feedback as to whether he/she kept the extensors flexed during loose in real time I am sure would work, but I don't see this being done for any but for the very elite. So, how do you train aspiring elite athletes to do this? I haven't a clue.

And I have to ask: if one doesn't have proof that this is a real and significant factor, should one advocate it?

Some clarification from the NTS camp is clearly needed.

Additional Learning References

Developing the Magic Release by Don Rabska (AFm, Vol 6, No 2)
My Second Second Chance by Brian J. Luke (AFm Vol 10, Nos 4 & 5)

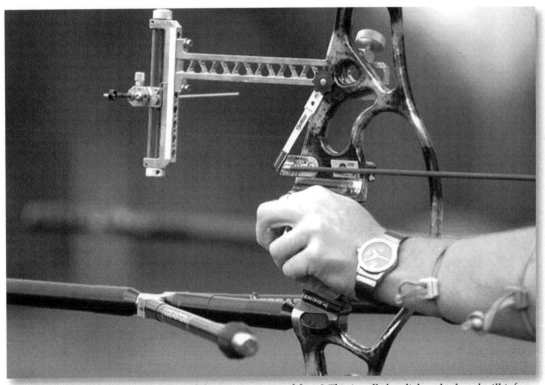

How far can you pull past your clicker while maintaining good form? This is called a clicker check and will inform you as to your clicker position as well as your potential consistency.
(Photo Courtesy of Andy Masdonald)

Chapter 3
Being Consistent

One of my students was complaining that during a 70m practice session he'd have one end of 8s, 9s, and 10s and then the next end would have 5s and 6s, but the following end was 8s, 9s, and 10s again. It was driving him nuts. Do you know what was going on with this student?

The problem of consistency is the bugaboo of archery. All kinds of people will tell you how to shoot and how to set up and tune your equipment, but few will tell you *how to be consistent*, which is the key aspect of scoring well. If you have nice, tight groups out in the six-ring, we can show you how to move it into the center. But if you are centered up and all over the place, or worse have alternating good and poor ends, what then?

Recurve Negotiations

The first point to recognize is that my archer has the capability to hold the 8-ring, the question is just (Just!) that he can't do it consistently. The general reason is he is asking his body to perform this task through athleticism rather than setting up his shot to repeat consistently. What I see most often in this situation is students with an incorrect draw length, typically too short. Consequently, if they draw smoothly and strongly to the anchor position their body can feel, they will zip right through their clicker. Their draws therefore become "negotiable." They draw looking for signals that their draw is "correct" (peeking at their clicker, "am I there, no, how about here?") and then they finish their shot. Some ends they are very good at doing this and they can shoot quite nice groups, but other ends they don't negotiate their draw length at all well, their rhythm is disrupted and, well, 5s and 6s happen, if not worse.

Generally I ask these students to do a "clicker check" (*see photo left*). If you are not familiar with this test, it is a way to determine if their clicker is close to where it should be. Have your archer set up to shoot an arrow, then tell him not to shoot the arrow; they will draw and hold but end with a letdown. What you ask him to do is when the clicker "clicks" to keep drawing, while holding onto their best full-draw body position. When their clicker clicks, I urge them to pull (Pull, pull, pull!) while checking to make sure their string isn't being pulled back along their face or other form flaws intruding. If the archer's form breaks down, it is a "do over." The point of their arrow should be able to get approximately one quarter of an inch (6mm) past the rear edge of their clicker, but no farther. If they can't get to one quarter of an inch past the clicker, the clicker is too far in. If they can pull past one quarter of an inch past the clicker, the clicker is too far out (by far the more common problem).

I have had students who could pull an inch and a half past their clickers! When we get their clicker properly placed, thus setting a correct draw length, their consistency is almost always better.

Why? Because the best full-draw body position is almost to the edge of the range of motion that we associate with a shot. The only reason we leave the quarter of an inch or so from the edge of our ability to draw the arrow back with good form is because we are not robots. We have days in which things are easy and others in which things are hard. I frequently refer to the "Bell curves" built into our body positions (and shot timing). Sometimes our elbow is exactly in line with the arrow at the loose, other times it is slightly ahead or slightly behind that position. What we want is for those Bell curves to be as narrow as possible and this comes from volume practice. But practice isn't enough.

Try shooting a bow from half draw. Even if you can set up a clicker to help you, you will find yourself having a very hard time of it. By building your shot to be right next to the edge of your range of motion, you can feel the uncomfortable tightness in your back muscles. You can feel the tightness in your bow side pectoral muscle. Those "feels" are what guide you to the spot you want to be in. There aren't good feelings to latch on to half way through a full power stroke. So, practice will not make perfect unless your shot is structured to make it so. I have a saying "you have to find your shot before you can own it." My student has physical problems that prevent him from getting to the perfect full-draw position so we had to build in a little bit of negotiation into his shot. Occasionally it is a little too much. We are working on what adjustments he can make.

Compounds, Too

You might not think compound archers could suffer from the same malady, but you would be wrong. The equivalent of a mis-set clicker creating a suboptimal draw length is a poorly set up bow. Because of the force-draw curve of compound bows, compound bows have a built-in draw length. If the bow's draw length setting doesn't perfectly match the archer's draw length then shots are going to be inconsistent (usually more so on the left-right axis). Once the draw weight is set to be comfortable, setting the draw length correctly is the next biggest (and very large) factor in allowing the archer to become consistent.

Please Show Me a Sign!

So, as a coach, do you just wait for your archers to complain to you about being inconsistent? Well, you might, if your goal was to be a rotten coach! You can and should anticipate this situation.

What to Look For Obviously if your archer is overbowed, consistency is not to going to happen, so if you see an archer struggling to draw his/her bow that is the first thing to fix. Second, you want to look at the archer's full-draw body position: for recurve archers you are looking for the Archer's Triangle; for compound archers you are looking for the Archer's Trapezoid (scapula line parallel to the arrow/string plane).

Compound archers want their elbow to be exactly in the string plane/behind the arrow at release. This means they are pulling straight back behind the arrow.

Recurve archers also want this position but if they can get their elbows around "past line," that is past being in line with the arrow/string plane, it is better as plucking the string becomes almost impossible. This is another example of setting up one's shot structurally to support consistency.

Some recurve archers will set up in a quite open stance as they have been told that that is the "correct" stance, but then can't get the shoulders in line 10°-12° closed to the target line which is what is needed to get into the Archer's Triangle. The solution is to close their stance until they can get into that good upper body position, then work on their trunk flexibility until they can have the stance they desire.

Conclusion

Consistency is not just the result of hours and hours of practice. The smart route involves setting up one's shot and equipment so that the body supports being in correct full-draw position. If you help your students do this they will become consistent more quickly and suffer less frustration along the way.

A Case Study

A recurve student who has been shooting compound (indoors) for about a year wrote me to ask:

Dear Coach Ruis,

This happens every time I practice compound: at the beginning of practice, my arrows land from 10 to 7. During the middle of practice, my arrows are extremely consistent, and I usually get 10 to 9. Then at the end of practice, my arrows are back to landing from 10 to 7. Is this diagnostic of anything?

❖ ❖ ❖

What do you think the source of his inconsistency is? (Yes, I know very little information was provided.)

Here is what I wrote back:

Can you characterize your misses (left-right or up-down)? It might be a matter of bow setup (centershot amongst other things).

This can be a matter of focus. At the beginning of practice you are just floating along and then you start catching those 7s, which stirs you to focus better. Later you get tired and lose focus again. It might also be a matter of conditioning, at least in part.

Also, don't be too quick to see a pattern. This is not an abnormal distribution. Are you logging your arrow scores? If not, I recommend you do so, but number your arrows and log the scores according to the sequence when shot. So, shoot the arrows in numerical order (#1, #2, etc.) and record the scores in numerical order (not just from greatest to least score). If for example, you are shooting too quickly, you will see the scores on your later arrows dip. If so, your "pattern" could be a matter of tempo. If in the middle of your session you shoot faster or slower than earlier and later, that might account for the score shifts.

As you can see, an archery shot has a lot of moving parts. Statistical analysis of results can only be effective if you are shooting consistently. Prior to that point you may be chasing ghosts.

Additional Learning References

Understanding the Bow Hand by Larry Wise (AFm, Vol 12, No 3)
You, Full Draw Position, and the Bow by Larry Wise (AFm, Vol 11, No 3)
The Lines of Archery by Steve Ruis (AFm, Vol 16, No 1)

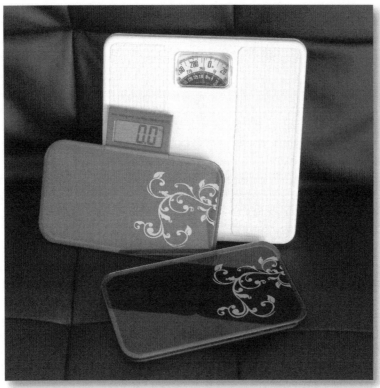

I tried electronic scales but they were too jumpy so I reverted back to plain, old bathroom scales (in back), which work well enough.

Chapter 4
Helping Your Student-Archers Explore Balance

If you haven't already addressed the importance of stance with your archers, you might want to do that first. Compare an archery stance (where the objective is to stand still) with golf and baseball stances (similar, but with more motion to support) and football and tennis stances (where the objective is to support movement in any direction).

After that, there are some things you can do to help your students explore the importance of balance in their shots. For one, during a practice, you can ask them to take a shot or two while standing on tiptoes. If that doesn't establish the importance of having good balance, nothing else will.

Exploring Balance

Larry Wise has a little drill he goes through with beginners to establish the balance in an archery stance. He asks them to stand with their feet together with their eyes closed and pay attention to how stable they feel. He then has them spread their feet out to approximately shoulder width and see, with their eyes still closed, how much more stable that stance is. This is certainly worth doing, don't you think?

Another simple drill is to have your student(s) stand with their feet close together and then lift one foot off of the ground. Tell them you are going to ask them to stand that way for a while, so be relaxed. Many will lose their balance in just a few seconds, others will be fine with that position for several minutes. All will experience the "balancing act," the slight shift in muscles that keep one's center of gravity vertically over their footprint (the condition for being balanced). The point of this drill is for your archers to feel those stabilizer muscles moving. Ask them if they think having those muscles shifting body parts around, however slightly is a good thing for an archer. They should all say "no."

Ask them to gauge, while standing on one foot, how much of their weight as a percent is on their heel (rear of the foot) and how much on the toes (front of the foot). The two numbers, of course, should sum to 100% representing all of their weight. (Any archer who has 40% on their heel and 27% on their toes has a math problem.) Ask them to keep the percentages to themselves. After everyone is done ask them to share their estimate for the amount on their toes (or heels, doesn't matter, but just one). The estimates are usually all over the place (75%, 35%, 50%, 25%, etc.) we will use these numbers later, so ask them to remember theirs.

Bring in the Bathroom Scales!

A First Experiment I use some inexpensive bathroom scales I picked up at IKEA for this (less than $10 each) as they are being used to help in a general sense, not to do scientific measurements. Two of these can be laid on the floor, bottom edge to bottom edge, so that a student can position their foot on it so their heel in on one and their toes on the other. A few pieces of plywood (or anything, really) can be stacked up next to these two scales for the other foot to stand on. It is nice if you have a couple of helpers from this point onward to read the scales. Ask each student to stand on the scales (left or right foot, but the same one for everybody) and the stack of wood (or whatever) the same height as the scales and take their archer stance. Ask them to close their eyes and get their weight as evenly distributed as they can, to get the feeling of being in balance. When they are ready, they say "now" and the two helpers read the scales.

After all of the rest have gone through, you can calculate what fraction of the total weight was on the toes and heels. (If you are a total geek, like me, you can set up a spreadsheet to do all of the calculations for you.) Ask them to compare what their actual weight distribution was with the one they estimated from the drill before.

Most students are pretty good at distributing their weight left foot and right, but they tend to overestimate how much weight is on their toes as compared with their heels.

You can expand this experiment by replacing the stack of wood with a third scale and have a third helper record that reading when the student-archer says "now." In this fashion you will get left-right as well as front-back scale readings and can share those data, too.

The upshot of this exercise is that students will realize that they can trust their sense of balance to distribute their weight appropriately for archery.

A More Advanced Experiment

For your more seasoned archers, there is another experiment you can do.

This involves using the three-scale setup as above, but once you get the baseline data, you repeat the measurements with a bow in hand. Actually I repeat this with the bow in hand two ways, one holding the bow in front of their bodies and two, at full draw. Since it can take a little time to feel whether one is balanced at full draw, and for recurve archers this may to a bit too long, I use a 10# draw bow with a heavy back weight screwed into the stabilizer hole (to simulate a real bow's weight a bit better).

So, do the baseline measurements as above, then hand them the bow, asking them to hold it close to their chest comfortably, and repeat the process. Then ask them to go to full draw and repeat again. (I tied a D-loop onto the bow string to accommodate release shooters.)

The upshot of this exercise is that the weight of the bow tends to shift a little more weight onto the toes (proportionately) both when just holding the bow and at full draw.

We also found that archers, especially experienced ones, accepted the weight of the bow almost entirely on the target-side foot when raising and extending the bow. Realize that at full draw, a substantial part of the weight of the bow is being held by the draw arm. Consequently the left-right balance (at or near 50-50) was preserved through the raise because at full draw it would be back close to what it was before the bow was raised, so why re-balance for the raise if you are just ending up pretty much back where you started at full draw?

Still More on Coaching Archery

Why We Want a Forward Weight Bias

The idea of an archer being balanced at full draw makes perfect sense. Any aspect of being out of balance will make aiming and execution more than a little uncertain. And once perfectly aligned with the target, we want to be able to stay in that position until the arrow is away because any movement moves us from perfect alignment to imperfect alignment. So, we want balance for the sake of stillness.

But holding several pounds of bow to one's side at arm's length has to be compensated for. This is done in two ways: one is by spreading one's feet far enough apart to provide some extra leverage. To see what I mean, try holding your bow at arm's length to the side with your feet side by side. Then spread your feet somewhat and you will find the task easier.

The second aspect of balancing an extended bow involves the assist one gets from the draw side. Since we are holding the bow on the bottom half, when we draw the bow we are pulling up a little when we are pulling back (*see the diagram*). The force from the center of pressure on the bow's grip back to the draw fingers or release aid has an "up" component that lessens the load on the bow arm due to gravity. And,

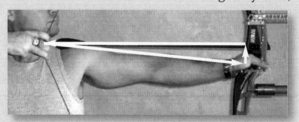

to some extent, the spreading of weight in the plane of the shot supplies stability like the long pole that tightrope walkers use.

But none of this produces any front-back stability; it is all in the archer's left-right directions, i.e. toward the target. By putting a slight amount of extra weight toeward on your feet, you build in a bias, a bias to fall forward! But this is a very tiny bias. At the same time, you engage muscles to keep you from falling and this actually makes your movements more predictable and less random. If you are perfectly balanced along an up-down (vertical) line, you are just as free to move left as right, front as back. In fact you are free to move in any direction. By leaning ever so slightly in one direction, you decrease the tendency to fall in any other direction and increase it in the direction of the lean, which actually makes it easier to stabilize your body's position. Consider a broom handle. If you stand it up against a wall flat, I can almost guarantee you it will fall over. If you pull the bottom end out a few inches from the wall and lean it against the wall, you have predisposed it to fall toward the wall, but the wall prevents it from doing so, so it is now much more stable than when it was put flat up against the wall, and far less likely to fall over. This is the same thing an archer does when he/she shifts his/her weight forward a tiny bit and then engages muscles to stop the fall.

But this doesn't answer the question of how much should be placed forward (55%, 60%, 67.8%?) nor does it help an archer find that "sweet spot" where they are most stable. If that could be measured, there should be a way to give archers feedback to help them find their most stable balance. No?

(adapted from **Even More on Coaching Archery**, 2013)

Conclusion

If there is a big "take away" it is that archers can trust their sense of being in balance to put them into the near optimal body positions needed for consistent, accurate shooting. Too often students interpret conditions like a "60%-40% weight balance" or "10%–70%–20% pressure balance on the fingers under their tab" as something they have to do, so they spend time trying to create those positions when in fact they are often best created in response to something else and not in isolation.

Coaches might want to dispense with prescriptions like these that sound like instructions but instead are descriptions. They are fine for coaches to talk about, but athletes might just be better off with statements like, "you want to feel in balance."

Additional Learning References

Your STANDing in Archery by Larry Wise (AFm, Vol 15, No 3)
Biomechanical Musings by Steve Ruis (AFm, Vol 13, No 2)
Whatever Happened to the Closed Statnce? by Steve Ruis (AFm, Vol 12, No 3)

Step 2
(Photo Courtesy of Ty Pelfrey)

Still More on Coaching Archery

Chapter 5
How to Build Championship Form

I've had a number of my athletes achieve state championship wins of late and I suspect that in some of them this accomplishment is going to stoke their competitive fire. So I am mulling over in my mind what I am going to do to help them build form and execution that results in consistent winning.

First, I examined the results (all the ITAA State Indoor Champions are determined by a 600 Round score at 18m but there is a 25m competition the next day, also). In the 18m competition there were 112 competitors and 77 medals were given out. This is pretty common in archery. The chances of winning a medal are often quite high (in this case there was an overall 69% chance of winning a medal). In addition, there were 23 shooting categories in which there were three or fewer competitors, which meant that if you finished you got a medal (100% chance of winning something). In some of those 23 categories (and some of the others) the top scorer crushed everybody else, so those top scorers had a 99+% chance of finishing first (and becoming state champion) as there was no real competition. By contrast, in the Compound-Senior-Male division, two archers (Tim Zimmerman and Brad Lasater) finished with identical scores of 576/600 and had the same numbers of 10s and the same numbers of 9s! This continued to a 29 to 28 shootoff victory. Now, that's competition!

I certainly would not point all of this out to my new winners. Talk about buzz kills. My philosophy is to allow them to enjoy those victories; if they get serious about winning, all of those realities will make themselves known.

Next, I want to avoid going "all in" or "whole hog" on them. The transformation of a quasi-recreational archer to a dedicated competitive archer isn't, in my opinion, an overnight conversion. I want to leave room to grow. If I overwhelm these student-archers with all the things they have to learn and do, archery might seem more like a job than a hobby. Nobody wants their hobby turned into a job, although there are plenty of examples of people who work far, far harder at their hobby than they do at their job. The effort they are willing to put forth is up to them and I think coaches will have a great deal more success if they feed their archers a bit, a digestible bit, at a time.

The Key is the Process
In my mind, I want to create a situation into which my athletes and I can incorporate

changes without significant disruption of the status quo. If every change in form required a complete rebuilding of the shot, how many archers would last through more than a couple of cycles of that? Not many, I think.

So there needs to be a process where new things get integrated fairly easily. It also needs to provide structure and direction. Most archery coaches aren't there for every single practice session to do this, so the athletes need to be able to do it for themselves. And if your archers aren't consumed by archery, they may not be accomplished practice planners—strike that—they *will not be* accomplished practice planners.

This process needs to involve all three phases of archery: form and execution (the physical aspects), equipment, and the mental aspects. Each of these requires constant, although not equal, attention. Initially archers focus on the physical execution issues, then they get involved in the equipment, and almost always consider the mental aspects last. This is not necessarily bad. If you look at the totality of these topics, there are several books worth of information that needs to be acquired and assimilated for each. Dumping all three on some hapless archer all at once is a recipe to create fisherman, as Bernie Pellerite says. So, a layered approach seems inevitable. And really this is how people learn: for example, we learn a little about the English language in the first grade, a little more in the second, more in the third, and we are still learning about it in college. (And I am still learning about it.)

My Best Estimate of Such a Process

The first person who reads this and says "Ruis says you gotta do it this way ..." is going to incur my wrath. In no way do I want to inhibit anyone's approach . . . but (and you knew that was coming, didn't you) . . . I think that we, collectively as coaches, need to be better organized. Having some structure, some processes available to you as a coach gives you something to work from, a place to start. For example, if you have an Olympic Recurve student who is having trouble with chest string clearance, what do you do? Do you have any idea? If you do, do you have any understanding of why that "solution" works? (I offered this "issue" as an example in that the standard treatment is to open the stance, which is bizarre, because "the archer's triangle" exists above the waist and if there is a problem there, something below the waist shouldn't be the solution.)

My feeling is that if you don't have to start everything from scratch, you can get farther than my generation of coaches did. (Starting every coach from scratch is not a recipe for progress and learning how to do things better.)

As always, what I offer is *a* way to do things, not *the* way.

Start With the Physical This is the way almost everybody gets started (Pull it back, let it go! Yeah!) and I believe it is a good thing. The reason is that archery is a repetition sport. Repeating doing it wrong not only doesn't help, it leads to the formation of bad habits that then take a great deal of effort to break. Not creating those bad habits is a huge advantage to your archers. So getting a shot close to being good at the get-go is quite important.

You've heard of the coaching dictum: *only work on one thing at a time*, yes? In my opinion that is only for intermediate archers and up. For beginners I will make so many corrections in one lesson that their heads spin. In fact, I don't want them to concentrate their attention on any one thing as a beginner. What I want to do is get them as close as I can to standard form as fast as I can. There is no benefit to them shooting with form far from what they will end up with—quite the reverse. So, I will correct everything without harping, with lots of encouragement, repetition, and praise for things done well. At this stage I don't care if they know the parts of the bow or the names of the phases of a shot, I only want them to be learning the safety rules and repeating fairly good shots.

My role is of the *Great Corrector*. I have to be careful to not come across as being negative, as asking for changes carries the implicit statement that "you are doing it wrong." So I am also the *Great Encourager*. Starting with a target up close (because they expect to be shooting at a target) so that their shots are successful (they have already defined "hitting the target" as a mild success and "hitting the center" as the ultimate success; you don't get to teach this or change it). The goal is "grouping" while the target is close up. Barriers to this goal are bows with too much draw weight, too much mass, and mismatched equipment that wouldn't give anybody reasonable results. (Note Program equipment that is lent to beginners is the definition of being mismatched; I mean fairly badly mismatched.)

Continuing with the Physical As soon as is practical, the Shot Sequence/Routine is introduced, which provides structure to both the physical and mental learning to come, and the transition to "only work on one thing at a time" is made.

Then Comes the Equipment If an archer never invests in his or her own equipment, you aren't training a competitive archer, so there is nothing further to tell them other than "Have fun . . . safely!" For the others, the acquisition of their own archery kit is the natural starting line on learning how to purchase, maintain, adjust, set up, and tune their equipment.

In all of our AER curricular materials we recommend this be done in stages, and most coaches do it this way. Unfortunately there isn't much help for this process. What does exist is scattered all over the place. I have told the story of the student we sent to our closest archery pro shop, with an exact list of what to get (at least the parameters) and especially who to talk to in the shop (we even included the phone number of the shop to call ahead to make sure the guy they needed was working that day). The excited teenager finally goaded his parent's into making the trip on a day our guy wasn't there and comes home with a bow physically too heavy and with 15# too much draw weight. But it was red and did have flames painted on the riser.

Even if you have a spectacular pro shop close by, with target archery specialists, it does not mean things will be easy (easier maybe, but not easy).

There are all kinds of good videos on YouTube and archery guides available free on the Internet, but everything is scattered all over the place and is hard to find. I collect this stuff up and supply it to my students, but it is hard to keep up and *they also find things on their own*. (**Warning**! If you were not aware of this, know that there is more inaccurate advice and crap on the Internet than there is good advice . . . lots more!) The stuff they find on the Internet might be good, but they don't have enough knowledge/discernment to sort the wheat from the chaff and students following such advice can create more problems than you can easily cure. I encourage my students to forward me anything they find interesting and think applies to them and I try to get back to them quickly as to whether it is good, in their case, or not.

Another reason it would be good to have a professional coaching association is to create instructional materials on basic archery gear that coaches can confidently steer their students toward. (If you don't think that's desirable, go on YouTube and search for "archery equipment" and see what you get.)

Again, it is important to layer the learning. Don't start with micro-tuning techniques. As I have said repeatedly, a good bow setup will serve a good long time with no tuning involved, so I begin with the elements of a good bow setup. Talk about handling and storing their equipment and maintaining it. And be ready for miscommunications. I saw a young compound archer setting up to shoot indoors and he took out a tube of wax and liberally waxed his bow string and cables. I asked him how often he waxed his string and cables and he said "Every time I shoot." It looked like he had a half a pound of wax on and in every crevice in his bow. He didn't know. He just heard that it was important to keep his strings "well waxed."

There is a lot to learn. Anything you can commit to paper and provide them to read on their own time is a good idea. If you supply it to them via email, you can include hot links to videos and written references from the Internet.

Finally Comes the Mental Now you've heard that it is never too early to start teaching the mental aspects of archery; you've probably heard that from me. But there is a problem. While I start on Day 1 addressing Self-Talk for example, I don't expect much learning to go on. The reason is that until they acquire some experience, there is no context for this information, so they don't have a reason to learn it. For example, one of my college archers emailed me (he had been shooting for about three years) that in a recent practice his arrows were almost all in the gold, but in his last practice he was having trouble holding the red (40cm target at 18m). "What was he doing wrong?" he asked. My response was "Welcome to archery!" and a beginning of a discussion: on normal variations in score, that as we progress our high and low scores on rounds get closer together and we become more consistent, but are never, ever perfectly consistent, that one needed to be constantly striving to improve, sometimes even to stay where we were score-wise.

If I were to try to teach this young man about the mental skills needed to achieve consistency would he have been able to absorb that information before he had noticed his own inconsistency? I think not.

So, I talk about things like self-talk, shooting "in the now," not thinking about score, etc. with up-and-coming archers but don't begin instruction on having a formal mental program until enough experience has been acquired to allow that learning, and in fact to encourage that learning. Until an archer has been taught to let down, and then used the Rule of Discipline (*If anything—mental or physical, anything at all—intrudes from a prior step or from outside the shot, you must let down and start over.*) for quite a while and experienced the fact that occasionally he will let down but not know why, will he really believe his subconscious mind monitors his shot so that he doesn't need to do that consciously?

So, yes, I believe that the mental game is a major key to success in competitive archery but I still start formal instruction on it with newly competitive archers last. The more important needs are experiencing good form, good grouping, learning the shot sequence, etc. so that the mental instruction strikes chords in their own experience. Otherwise it is all airy-fairy stuff that doesn't seem to apply to them.

Is There More to Come?
You bet your bippy, Bubba! I got the feeling this may just be Part 1.

Additional Learning References
Zone Mechanics by David Clink (AFm, Vol 10, No 5)
Teaching or Coaching? by Tim Scronce (AFm, Vol 10, No 3)
Shot Planning by Steve Ruis (AFm, Vol 16, No 3)
Do You Practice with a Plan? by Tom Dorigatti (AFm, Vol 13, No 3)
An Intermediate Fitness Plan by Annette Musta (AFm, Vol 7, No 4)
Better Accuracy Through Better Bow Selection by Larry Wise (AFm, Vol 15, No 4)

Now these archers are relaxed!
(Photo Courtesy of Andy Macdonald)

Still More on Coaching Archery

Chapter 6
Relaxing

I have a student who has Olympic Recurve ambitions and he took his first trip to the Arizona Cup recently. He struggled on the first day with getting through his clicker (it is quite windy there). He called me that night and we made adjustments and he ended up tied for seventeenth place, which I think was quite a good outcome.

Back at practice, his obvious question was "why did I struggle with the clicker?" My response was simple: tension. Since wind is seldom steady and completely uncontrollable, it can create a great deal of anxiety: Am I going to get this shot off in time? Is it going to score well? Should I let down . . . again?

Muscle tension shortens muscles, shortens your draw stroke, and thus makes getting through the clicker harder. Striving harder to get through the clicker creates more tension, which makes it even harder . . . this is a positive feedback loop!

The obvious fix is to relax the muscles involved, but just how do you do that?

Relaxing

Muscles are normal controlled autonomically or unconsciously but can be flexed consciously, *e.g.* bodybuilders pose: biceps flexed, not flexed, flexed, not flexed. But is "not flexed" the same as "relaxed?" I think it is not so. Muscles seem to be able to go through long transitions during which they are neither totally flexed nor totally relaxed. Body builders talk about the "pump" in which, through a number of flexes, a muscle can be increased in size as if it were being pumped up. This increase in the amount of flex is also an increase in muscle tension. As it applies to archery, it clearly is necessary to avoid the "pump" from one shot to another in a long end (five or six arrows) which is exacerbated by nervous tension.

There is a surprising amount of information on relaxing. How scientific the "research" behind this is is debatable. My point is if you do an Internet search on that topic, be ready for a flood of hits. I will try to simplify this by addressing two (quite probably oversimplified) approaches to relaxing muscles: muscle-to-brain and brain-to-muscles.

Muscles-to-Brain Relaxation Techniques

Controlled Breathing Possibly the most common relaxation techniques tap into breathing patterns. In fact, your breathing patterns are strong indicators of your state of tension, so your awareness sphere as an archer needs to be expanded to include your breathing (if it hasn't been already). Obviously this attention must be embedded unconsciously, as conscious thoughts about breathing will interfere with your shot.

When you are calm, confident, and in control of your shot, breathing is slower, deeper, and less noticeable. When you are feeling the pressure and become tense, your breathing becomes faster, more shallow, and more noticeable (but something you still might not notice because of your focus on the competition).

Ideally your breathing will be linked to your shot, centered upon the draw (look up info on archer's breathing patterns—there is no right or wrong as we are all different, what we are striving for is linkage which makes us more consistent).

In the simplest terms, breathing in tends to make us more tense while breathing out makes us more relaxed. This is why heavy exertion athletes (weight lifters, baseball pitchers (during a pitch), tennis players (during a stroke), etc.) tend to breathe out while at maximum exertion.

Deep Breathing One simple relaxation technique is deep breathing. This is simply filling your lungs to their maximum extent and then exhaling. With practice a simple repetition can become a trigger for effective relaxation. Deep breathing relaxes shoulder and neck muscles in particular, so is good for archers, and also provides a mental break in the sequence of executing good shots. Back before I had asthma, I did this in reverse: forced exhalation followed by relaxed inhalation. This had the novelty of being different from normal breathing and because I did it to relax, it became associated with being relaxed, which I think helped it be a useful technique for me.

Slow Breathing Research has shown (Williams and Harris, 1998) that breaths in which the exhale takes twice as long as the inhale (often called "1:2 breathing") are particularly effective in creating relaxation. This can be combined with deep breathing.

Yawning I have heard this also called a "fake yawn." In any case you just simply execute a long, drawn-out yawn. This takes just a few seconds. Since yawning is associated with boredom and unexciting situations, body and mind respond in that direction. Try it; I have and it works.

Smiling Like yawning, effecting a big smile can induce relaxation. This is also a form of mood shifting (*see below*).

Relaxation Training This may seem a little far-fetched but it seems to work. There are relaxation scripts, which when followed lead to relaxation (*see the sidebar right for one such*). Many focus on the deliberate flexing of muscles and their subsequent relaxation, which is just what we want. Such scripts and the directed exercises are just a way of reminding ourselves that "this is flexed" and "this is relaxed" and that we want "relaxed." This is often called "relaxation response" training. If you follow such a script for a time (I have done so) you can then trigger the whole response with just a part of it, such as crimping and relaxing your toes.

If you want access to such a pool of relaxation, you must adopt a script (the Internet is full of them if you don't like the example below), use it regularly, and then research which part of it triggers the effect of the whole (or at least much of it).

Brain-to-Muscles Relaxation Techniques

Here are a number of short techniques (short to allow their use on the shooting line) that start with thoughts and lead to muscle relaxation.

Imagining You Are Elsewhere If you feel tense, imagine that you are shooting in your

Still More on Coaching Archery

Progressive Muscle Relaxation Model Script

Make yourself comfortable either sitting upright in a chair, or lying down. Close your eyes, relax and take a deep breath in. Slowly breathe out as you expel the worries from your mind. Maintain this breathing pattern throughout the exercise, breathing in relaxation and breathing out any tension. Take another deep breath in and let it out, telling yourself "I am relaxed and calm."

In this exercise you will relax each muscle group from head to toe, beginning with the upper body. Try to focus on the way your muscles feel, and the relaxation that you experience.

Face—Tighten the muscles of your face by making a grimace, squeezing your eyes shut, and wrinkling your forehead. Hold the contraction and feel the tension. . ., and now release. Feel the difference in your muscles that are now relaxed.

Neck—Bend your neck by tilting your head to your left shoulder. Feel the tightness through the side of your neck. Return to the center, and now tilt your head to your right shoulder. Again, notice the tension in the side of your neck. Return to the center, and notice that the tension is now released. Take a deep breath in, and slowly let it out. Next, tilt your head back. Hold this, and now relax. Bend your neck forward, as if to touch your chin to your chest. (Pause.) Slowly lift your head back to its normal position, noticing your neck feels tall and strong.

Shoulders—Pull your shoulder blades back towards each other. Then release, as you return your shoulders to their normal position. Now curve your back by rolling your shoulders forward. Hold the contraction, and relax. Next, arch your back, feel the tension, and relax. Shrug your shoulders as if to touch your ears. Hold the tension, and release the stress.

Take a deep breath in, hold it, and now release. Feel yourself breathing in relaxation, and breathing out tension.

Upper chest—Take another deep breath in, feeling your chest and abdomen expand. Hold the breath in, feeling the stretch in your muscles. Now slowly exhale and feel your muscles relax as your stomach falls.

Abdomen—Tighten your abdominal muscles. Feel the tightness of your muscles. Now relax.

Arms—Tense your upper arms by bending at the elbow and flexing your bicep muscle. Notice the contraction and the tension in your arms. Slowly unfold your arms and relax. Clench your fists, hold, and now release the tension.

Hands—Firmly press your fingertips into your palms by bending at the knuckle. Feel the tension in your hands. Slowly uncurl your fingers. Now just lightly touch your fingertips to your palms. Hold this, and relax.

Take a deep breath in, telling yourself, "I am relaxed and calm." Hold it, and now exhale any tension in your body. Take one more deep breath in, and let it out.

Buttocks—Squeeze your buttock muscles together. Hold the tension, and now release the stress.

Thighs—Focus on your legs. Contract your thigh muscles tightly. Now relax them, and notice the feelings in your leg muscles. Now contract them again, this time with only half of the intensity. Let go of the contraction, and release the stress.

Calves—Next, tense your calf muscles by pointing your toes out in front of you. Hold the contraction. Now slowly release the tension, returning your foot to a comfortable position. Point your toes toward the ceiling to contract the calf muscles again, but this time with less intensity. Hold this. Now relax the muscles and feel the tension leaving your legs.

Feet—Curl your toes under as tightly as you can, and hold the contraction. Concentrate on the tense feeling in your toes and feet. Now release the stress.

Feel the contrast in your muscles from when you started the exercise. Notice that your muscles are now completely relaxed.

Take a deep breath in. Hold it, and release. Open your eyes, and feel the relaxation in your muscles. Notice how refreshed and energized you feel. Begin to think about what you will do when you finish this exercise, and what the rest of the day holds. Continue to breathe in relaxation and breathe out tension. When you are ready, slowly get up out of your chair, stretch if you need to, and go on with your day.

most comfortable venue (your basement, garage, back yard, home range, etc.). The more vivid you can make this imagery, the more effective it will be at relaxing your muscles.

Mood Shifting This is just deliberately yanking (sliding, nudging, etc.) yourself into a more positive mood. I used the word yanking because my trigger is the thought "you are better than this" and I have an image of picking myself up by the scruff of my neck and giving myself a good shake (to shake myself out of the fear of failure or embarrassment that typically drives my mental tension). You may prefer different energy/imagery but the idea is to consciously shift one's mood to something more productive. Here, "different" can be as good as "better," as tension is often generated by competition pressures or environmental conditions (wind, rain, etc.) and anything that breaks the negativity of your thinking that is creating unwanted tension can work.

Pace Control Often when we get anxious, we speed up our shooting. If you notice you are shooting faster (and faster), slow down! You may want to look into ways to control the pace/tempo of your shot (metronomes, song lyrics, etc.). I teach beginning serious archers to always begin their shooting warm-ups with a couple of letdowns, followed by shots at 85% of normal speed rising to 100% by their sixth arrow or so. This (without the letdowns) is also their first level disaster recovery technique. If they lose their shot or confidence in their shot and there is no equipment failure or environment reason, this is how to regain control. Starting with a slightly slower, more focused shot, they regain rhythm quickly thereafter. Obviously if you were shooting too fast, this will break that tendency. You may want to begin your shooting warm-ups with the same "disaster recovery" routine. Doing so means your recovery program is recently practiced and easy to slide into.

I recommend avoiding really slow, deliberate shooting (except as a training exercise), really anything less than 85% of normal pace, as this is too far removed from the pace of the huge log of good shots you have recorded in memory. And it practically invites intrusions of conscious thoughts into your shot process.

As with all such techniques, they must be practiced to be effective.

Additional Learning References

Take a Deep Breath by Alison Rhodius (AFm, Vol 12, No 6)
Remember to Breathe by Leighton Tyau (AFm, Vol 9, No 5)
The Re-interpretation of Anxiety by Alison Rhodius (AFm, Vol 8, No 6)
Relaxation is the Target by Lisa Franseen, Ph.D. (AFm, Vol 1, No 3)

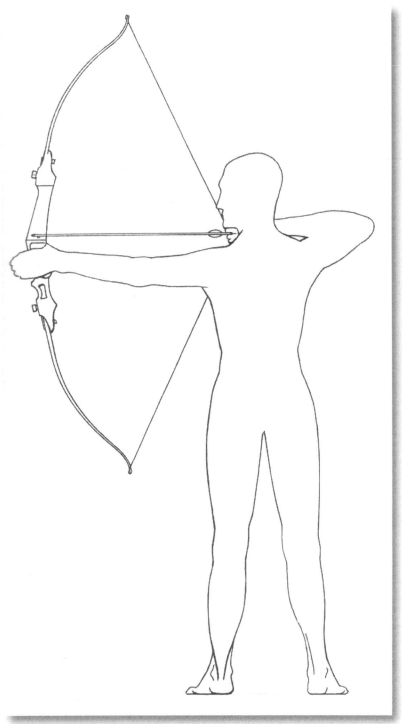

Ah, the archer with perfect form, but who is this hollow man?

Chapter 7
The Physical Requirements
of a Good Shot

The Requirements Begin with the Bow

Bows are simple machines. Recurve bows and longbows accept human energy in the form of bent/stressed limbs that then, through their own resilience, transfer that energy to an arrow using the string that was used to deform the limbs. Even compound bows follow this simple formula. The vertical plane, including the arrow and which roughly is the same plane that the string moves in, determines the left-right attitude of launched arrows. To receive a full measure of energy from the bow and to be able to fly into the target center, the arrow must reside in, or be very near to, that vertical plane when it is aligned with target center. The archer's body must hold the bow so that the arrow is in that position. Anything that moves the bow away from that position increases the error of the shot. Period. Full stop.

Plus Archery is a Repetition Sport

As archery is a repetition sport, meaning you must do the same thing over and over with the same or a similar outcome, bell curves are important. You may remember bell curves from school; for example the typical grading "curve" is a bell curve. It is called a "bell" curve not because a guy named Bell invented it, but because of its shape. Many of the bell curves in archery need to be small, very small. For example, Rick McKinney once determined that the difference between a score of 9 or 10 at 90m in the old Olympic competitions was less than a sixteenth of an inch at the arrow head. Consequently archers must find that position and hold still in that position because moving back and forth through a wide spread injects timing into the shot, which has its own bell curve. (Bernie Pellerite calls these "drive-by shootings.")

This is why clickers are used almost universally in Olympic Recurve now when they were not 50 years ago. In the absence of clickers, some full draw positions differed from others in the extent of the draw. This spread might be $\frac{3}{16}''$ or it might be $\frac{1}{2}''$ or even more. Since draw length determines the spine match of bow and arrow, and an inch of draw is often the difference between one spine group and another, this is a significant source of variation. A clicker can reduce the size of these bell curves to an almost negligible amount (almost, but not quite)

So, archers must control their body positions in space in order to control the positions of their bows and arrows but also need to control their positions in time. Shots held a little too long or not quite long enough often score poorly. The regularity of the shots of elite archers is really quite astonishing.

An Archer's Positional Requirements

Stance Descriptions about how to shoot usually start with the stance, but that is backward for our purposes. We are looking for a stance that supports the arrow being held so as to be able to fly into the target center. If we "select" or "decide" on a particular stance, we may inhibit this process. Obviously, if we are training a brand new archer, we place them into a stance that is guaranteed to give them a reasonable chance of learning to shoot well, but the odds that that stance is what they will end up with are rather poor.

Consider this technique. Have the archer stand on a large turntable (*aka* Lazy Susan). Have them draw and anchor comfortably. The rotate the turntable until the archer's arrow is in the vertical plane going through target center. Voila! That is the archer's stance (really just the foot positions).

The point of this rather silly exercise is that the stance must support the archer's full-draw body position. An easier approach is to have the archer stand on the shooting line and draw and anchor with his/her eyes closed. If, when the archer opens their eyes, their sight aperture or arrow point isn't in the vertical plane including the target center, they shuffle their feet until it is. Then they repeat. They do this until when they open their eyes their arrow is properly positioned. (*Note* This exercise is a fool's errand if the archer's upper body position is flawed or inconsistent.)

From this "natural stance" an archer may choose to open or close their stance to acquire some benefit, stability on a windy day, for example. But such adjustments are not to sacrifice certain things, like: balance, internal stability, or upper body geometry.

Balance is determined by the spread of the stance (typically shoulder width at the heels) and the rotation of the feet/legs. Internal stability refers to the ability to hold a stable, that is non-moving (still!), body posture that supports the arrow being in the proper plane and the archer being able to loose the string without moving the bow or changing the normal string path. Upper body geometry refers to the bracing required to hold the bow and arrow still at full draw (*e.g.* archer's triangle or archer's trapezoid).

Whatever is done with the stance, if it detracts from the above, the cost is probably too high for whatever benefit is envisioned.

Many things are not even considered for part of an archer's stance because of the obvious negative consequences, like standing tiptoe (massive loss of balance) or standing with your bow side foot behind the shooting line and draw side foot in front (pointed the wrong way). But whatever is considered, the above factors need to be maintained.

The Draw Many older books on archery instruction refer to the draw as the "preeminent" or "most important" step in archery form. It is not . . . but you need to realize that because of a dearth of instruction, people were doing some really weird things to draw their bows. Many, being overbowed, were challenged to get the string back at all, which led them to stamping their lead foot, for example. Other adaptations included drawing up or drawing down or drawing while winding up like a baseball pitcher.

A major problem in recreational archery now (as then) is archers being overbowed, leading them to some of these flawed draws (especially drawing down, which is holding the bow overhead and drawing while the bow is moving down). If an archer is overbowed, they cannot draw safely, so they must drop down in draw weight until they can. Later, they can train to be able to use a higher draw weight if that is desirable.

The draw is the only large-scale motion after the bow is raised. (I use the raising of the bow as the start of a shot, because prior to that point timing is not critical, but after that point the timing of the shot becomes very important.) Because it is a large-scale motion, it takes some seconds for the effect of that motion to die down, that is for you to become still. (With kids, I use the cartoon example of a running character vibrating to a stop—think of the Road Runner.) Consequently we want the draw to be smooth. If we jerk the bowstring back we need a great deal more time at full draw to check to see if everything is in the right position and is still before loosing and time at full draw is a precious commodity. We also see secondary problems like arrows falling off of rests, hand positions on string and riser changing, etc.

If, on the other hand, we draw very slowly we are wasting time under the stress of the draw, which equates to a waste of energy. We want the draw to accelerate smoothly at the start and decelerate smoothly at the end. I teach my students to position their sight apertures at the end of the "raise" so that when the draw is complete and anchor position adopted, the aperture is on target center. This prepositioning of the aperture can be found by simple experimentation. The purpose of it is to conserve time (and therefore energy) at full draw. Waste energy and you will get tired earlier and fatigue will most definitely cost you points. This is true during a single shot as well as a long (5 or 6 arrow) end, as well as a whole round of a tournament.

The Loose There is a rather accomplished young archer in this area who shoots both compound and recurve. His scores with his compound bow are higher than his scores with his recurve bow. This is somewhat general assuming an equal amount of attention is paid to each bow. The primary difference and cause for the score difference is the use of a release aid with the compound bow. If this young man were to shoot his compound bow with a finger release, I expect his scores would be very similar to those with his recurve bow.

A mechanical release aid, if used properly, gives a cleaner loose of the string than does a finger release. The word "cleaner" means "with less variation," that is a smaller bell curve of release conditions (positions and angles).

The finger release of the string is a nonevent; it is caused by simply ceasing to hold the string back. In both finger release technique and mechanical release technique, we want to avoid the release becoming something you do, rather than something that happens due to other things being done. The finger release is trickier as it is often slaved to a clicker (although not to the level of being a conditioned reflex).

The major activity during the loose that does not seem to get enough attention is the change in load of the bow arm. Because the center of pressure of the bow hand is on the grip below the bow's center (the center is typically at the pivot point), the draw arm is pulling back on the string but, in effect, both upward and backward on the bow. This upward component of the draw force can support a significant amount of the bow's weight against gravity. But when the loose happens, the bow arm alone is suddenly supporting the entire weight of the bow. Since the arrow only takes about 0.015 seconds to leave the string, the bow cannot fall far during that time – but it will fall, and because it does it has it's own bell curve as to how far it will fall. Since the bow is presumed to be in perfect position at the beginning of the loose, falling means moving it into a less-than-perfect position.

Consequently, archers are taught to "hold the bow up" through the followthrough. This bracing of the bow arm must be learned; it does not come naturally. If an archer becomes accustomed to letting the bow fall after loosing, then another bell curve comes into play, this one involving time. Sometimes the bow falls after the arrow is away and sometimes just before (the dreaded "dropping your bow arm" form flaw).

The Followthrough The followthrough happens after the arrow is gone so it cannot affect the score of the arrow, so why is so much time spent discussing it? The reason is this: if the archer can avoid doing anything other than bracing their bow arm, and all other elements of the bow arm (wrist and hand) are kept relaxed, the behavior of the bow at that point forward is determined by the forces that were/are acting on it. If shot after shot the followthrough is the same, the archer is being consistent. If the bow bounces a different way in the hand or if the stabilizer swings in a different arc, something different was done. From the motion of the bow, the errant force can be identified and corrected. But if the bow arm is dropped or the hand moved purposely, this information can be obscured.

So a consistent followthrough is an indicator of consistent forces acting on the bow at and forward in time from the loose.

So, Shots Have to Be Done Right . . . Right?

No, shots do not need to be done "right." If this were true then you would see everybody in the same style shooting with identical or near identical form and they don't. Often champion archers show quite idiosyncratic form. The basic point here is that if any element of an archer's form is suboptimal for that archer, there is a cost associated with that. Some of these things can be paid for as an extra training cost, others are too expensive because of massive score costs (like having your feet on the wrong side of the shooting line) but those tend to get weeded out.

There is no such thing as one "correct" form: it is either suitable to an archer or it is not. What we call "correct" or "textbook" form is just our attempts to describe an ideal form that satisfies the physical requirements for good shots. Most archers have physical impediments or mental impediments preventing them from doing this form exactly. Plus, few teachers/coaches provide clear pathways to that form. You cannot take a youth with a youth's musculature and mentality and get them to adopt elite archer form and execution. They are neither physically nor mentally up to those tasks. So, they must be brought along in a series of stages, which over time and with practice, can morph into that elite archer form, while providing satisfaction/success to the archer along the way.

Additional Learning References
Following Up on Following Through by Steve Ruis (AFm, Vol 15, No 6)
Where Form Flaws Come From by Steve Ruis (AFm, Vol 11, No 3)
Biomechanics Basics by Steve Ruis (AFm, Vol 11, No 3)
Teaching Form by Steve Ruis (AFm, Vol 9, No 5)

Would one of these help you find your ideal rhythm?

Still More on Coaching Archery

Chapter 8
We Don't Talk Nearly Enough About . . .
Stillness and Rhythm

Stillness

Imagine yourself at full draw. You are in The Zone; everything is effortless. You know that this arrow is going into target center. You are at peace. Now, I ask you: would you be better off if you were swaying back and forth? How about to and fro? How about any movement at all? I think it is clear that we intuitively believe that we will shoot better if we are still at full draw.

Not only that, but we want to minimize the necessary motion associated with the execution of the shot as it continues. If we are perfectly aligned with the target and we move, we change from that perfect alignment to a less-than-perfect alignment and that is not conducive to higher scores. We know this from history. When release aids were popularized during the recurve era, archers immediately realized that their scores with their recurve bows were going up. The reason: less movement associated with the string being loosed.

This issue came up from reflection upon the myriad students I have worked with who pause little or not at all after hitting their full-draw-position. In order to determine if we are still/not moving, we need more than a snapshot of time. A photo of a runner with a fast enough camera freezes that runner in space so it looks as if he is not moving. If you don't allow enough time for a movement to be seen, you won't see it.

This is complicated by the fact that we are not ever really still. I was shown an interesting experiment as a young man. If you stand on a high quality mechanical bathroom scale, you will notice that the needle indicating your weight wiggles back and forth in a steady rhythm. If you count the number of wiggles per minute, you will discover that it is exactly the same as your heart rate. As your heart beats, it pushes a significant volume of blood out of one area in your body into another. This results in a slight shift in our center of mass and creates the equivalent of us jumping up and down on the scale (a tiny bit).

We are never really still.

So, at full draw we are not just pausing to see if we are either "moving" or "not moving" (still), we are checking to see if we are moving at our minimum level, which takes even more time to determine. So, if you have snap-shooting youngsters or even adults who spend way too little time at full draw, you now know what they need to pause for (at least part of it).

For the really young ones, I use the metaphor of cartoon characters who "vibrate" to a stop after running (e.g. Road Runner). Since the "hold" in the shot follows a quite large-scale motion (the draw), we need to take a second or so to let the residual movements die down.

Rhythm

Archery is a repetition sport. For our newbies we always acknowledge their first bull's-eye (at the least we would sing the (ABC) Olympic theme fanfare (Dah, dah, da-dah, dah, dah, dah…, sometimes we even gave out bull's-eye medals or stickers). The second time they did it was more like "That's nice; now do it again."

One of the key components to consistency is shooting in rhythm. Why this is so, I can't prove, but I think your own experience would support this. If you find yourself shooting too slowly or too quickly, at least compared to your normal rhythm, you would probably also find your arrow scores suffering.

"Okay," you say, "so it's fine. I need to pay attention to my rhythm, now what?"

Well, the problem is, everybody talks about it but nobody does anything. It's as if it were the weather. Let's look a little closer at shooting rhythm.

Inside Rhythm Archery is a repetition sport, more so than about any other sport. So, you shoot an arrow, shoot another, and shoot another. If the conditions are the same, each of those shots would score better if shot the same way than if shot X different ways. If the conditions change then adjustments need be made, but if not, just repeat the successful shot you just made. (Research shows that it is easier to repeat a motion just made than to do one from scratch.) Golfers, too, are in a repetition sport: they hit the ball, then hit it again, and again. But each shot is quite different from the last (except for rare exceptions). Hit the ball hard and it lands on the green, at which point you are tapping the ball rather than hitting it hard again. In target archery, you may shoot the exact same shot dozens of times from the exact same spot under virtually the same conditions. The extreme example is the indoor target archer: the environmental conditions are essentially constant.

Each of those shots is a sequence of activities and research has shown us some things about how we learn sequential tasks, like tying our shoes. Using brain scanners we have been able to determine that when first learning a string of tasks, there are substantial delays between those linked activities. (If you watch a three-year-old learning to tie his own shoes you will see this.) As the sequence is practiced, the amount of mental effort going into each activity stays roughly the same, but the waiting periods between them shrink and shrink. As it is said: one thing leads to another. An example of this is an experience we have all had (at least if you are of a certain age). When you were younger, you had a favorite album/CD that you played to death and then later, you picked up a "greatest hits" collection of that same group. When you inserted the CD in your player, you heard the first tune and enjoyed it but the next tune gave you a mild shock. It was the wrong song. Your brain was expecting the one that came after that first song on the *original* album.

Not only that but if you had that original album and started to play it, I could ask you at the beginning of Track 3, say, "What's the next track?" and you would struggle to remember it. But if I asked you "What's the next track?" near the end of Track 3, you would struggle much less to recall it. The reason is you don't need to know or anticipate what the next track is until you get close to the end of the one you are listening to. This is called "linking" and it is the basis for "one thing leads to another" in repetitive tasks. The *end* of one task is linked to the *beginning* of the next. When you have your shot "down," one thing leads right into the next with no pauses.

So, do you have such a shot?

Finding Rhythm I have been working with a student whose one and only problem right now is rhythm. Some shots take 13 seconds, others five (from bow raise to loose). When he is shooting "well" he tends to shoot quickly and easily. When he starts to struggle, shot times get longer and more irregular and letdowns proliferate.

With a little judicious use of a stopwatch and a lot of talk we think we have located the hang-up. There was one spot in his shot where the delay seemed to be occurring. When we addressed it we realized that the problem was that there was no link there. One thing did not lead to another and he ended up waiting for something to happen instead of triggering the next thing in line. We don't know if the problem is solved (that's going to take more time) but his shots had a lot more flow to them after we worked to create a mental link for the spot missing one.

Going with the Flow What I want to see is a shot that flows. Some people shoot more quickly and others more slowly, but there should be a flow, and the tempo of that flow consistent. The speed with which an arrow is loaded should be the same tempo as the bow is raised and the string is drawn. It is hard enough being consistent with one tempo; I can't imagine trying to keep a half dozen of them in line.

I am coming to the realization that the shot really starts when the bow is raised. From that point in time, maintaining tempo is critical. If your pre-shot routine is a little slower or a little faster, it doesn't matter so much. (Check out a golfer's practice swings or a baseball batter's practice swings; they are almost never at the same tempo as their actual swings.) But I think archers will benefit from a tempo match and linkage between the pre-shot routine and the shot. The loading of an arrow, the setting of the hands, the visualization of a perfect shot: if these are at a markedly different tempo than the shot itself, how does that help? But if they are both done at about the same speed there is a rhythm, a tempo, that carries you along and, well, one thing leads to another, and if you can keep it going, I have to believe that you will be more consistent in your grouping. And that is rarely a bad thing.

Additional Learning References

Shot Tempo Training by Van Webster (AFm, Vol 12, No 4)
Aiming Better by Larry Wise (AFm, Vol 15, No 5)

Is it now? Is it coming? Did we pass it?

Still More on Coaching Archery

Chapter 9
What Is the Most Important Part
of an Archer's Form?

Okay, coaches, if you're reading this you probably already have an answer to the question posed by the chapter's title, so what is it? Is it the stance? Is it the release? Is it getting the draw elbow "in line?" It seems that everyone has an opinion. But is this discussion going anywhere? Should we even be engaging in it?

The Reality of the Situation
Obviously any part of a shot can be done wrong. Some parts have more dire consequences than others when done wrong. The earlier steps in the shot sequence have a greater capability of messing things up simply because they come "before" other steps. If you mess up your stance, can you correct for it later on? Obviously this depends on the magnitude of the mistake. If your bow side foot is behind the shooting line and your draw side foot is ahead of the shooting line, you are in trouble so deep there is nothing you can do. If your stance is normally 12° open and for your next shot it is 13° open, maybe there is no problem at all.

When I was teaching experimental science I went to great lengths to distinguish between mistakes and errors—a mistake being something you did wrong and could do over correctly, but an error is a small variation in process that cannot be eliminated. Every part of a shot has errors associated with it, small variations in body position and execution from shot to shot. These cannot be eliminated, only minimized. Mistakes, on the other hand, we can deal with . . . if (and it is a big "if") we notice them. The usual procedure when we do is "to let down and start over."

So, Which Part of the Shot . . .
Some say that having a strong bow arm is 60% of the quality of a shot. I say, "So what?" If you have a strong bow arm, but a weak release, does the strong bow arm compensate for the weak release? I don't think so. Having strong parts is a good but the adage is that "a chain is only as strong as its weakest link" not "as strong as its strongest link."

My point is that to the archer-athlete these questions are nonsensical. The archer-athlete needs to know what it is they need to work on. There seem to be two approaches to this:

Work On Your Weak Points to Make Them Strengths This is a generally accepted approach, adopted by coaches in many sports. When Michael Jordan entered the NBA, the weakest part of his game was shooting. By the end of his career, he was a very good shooter. Mr. Jordan, you can be sure, spent a great deal of time working on his shooting. Sergio Garcia of Spain, a professional golfer, was ranked very low in putting, which he felt was holding him back. He worked very hard on his putting and now is ranked near the top in that aspect of his game. There are myriad other examples. Turn your weaknesses into strengths. While we all have limitations, modern studies indicate that almost any weakness can be addressed and significantly improved through dedicated practice.

Work on Your Strengths and Your Weak Points Will Take Care of Themselves This approach, advocated by Coach Kim of Korea amongst others, takes the approach that if you dwell on your weak points it strengthens them. After all, there is an adage that says "what you oppose, you make stronger."

This is not so broadly accepted as an approach to strengthening weak aspects of oneself or one's craft, but whichever approach is tried, it must be committed to. You do not want to waffle back and forth between these two approaches.

As a General Approach

Clearly, the most important part of an archer's shot is the part being done at that very moment. All focus and concentration must be upon the "now," that is to be focused on what it is they are doing right then and on nothing else. The real issue is "on what must we focus to shoot a consistent, excellent shot?" This is the true role of the shot sequence, not some distraction for one's conscious mind.

Each of the elements of an archer's shot sequence, including the sub-elements, must be focused on in turn, otherwise something could be done incorrectly or out of sequence. So, every archer's sequence must be built (the sheet music for a shot isn't a given) and then detailed so a complete list of items must be created and which then becomes the basis for focusing in "the now" on one's shot. Sticking to one's own sequence is important because if variations are allowed, then "improvisations" will pop up when the archer is under competition pressure. And we don't want to be making up new ways to shoot, on the fly, during competitions.

A key element in learning this is what I call the Rule of Discipline: *If anything—mental or physical, anything at all—intrudes from a prior step or from outside the shot, you must let down and start over.* This is the core practice for creating "dedicated practice" that maximizes progress and learning. No mistake goes uncorrected. No bad shots are willingly taken. You shoot your sequence and only your sequence.

And If I Fail. . . ?

And if some aspect of an archer's shot is clearly weak.? Then you will have identified a major source of imprecision, of why their groups are larger than they or you think they should be. In the case of one of my students, each step was done very well and all steps were at the same level of accomplishment, but the time these steps took was wildly inconsistent. This created a large scoring deficit. This is what we are working now to correct.

Whether your choice is to work to strengthen that weak shot element directly (the "strengthen your weaknesses" approach) or not (the "strengthen your strengths" approach), you now have an idea of what to check to see if you are making progress.

In defense of the "strengthen your strengths" approach, sometimes just the desire for something to get better unleashes subconscious mechanisms to make it so. (Ah, sweet mysteries of life!)

And, All Together Now

When I watch elite archers shoot, I see incredible fluidity and regularity. It looks so easy. One needs to avoid too much focus on "parts" without a regard for the "whole." My student with the timing problem is struggling with creating a repeatable, regular "whole" out of quite excellent parts. So, even if you identify a weak "part" of your or a student's shooting, always realize that you not only want that part to improve but you want it also to play well with the other parts. Just as a musician who looks good while playing crappy music is unacceptable, an archer who looks good while getting crappy scores is equally unacceptable. The purpose of breaking shots into parts is not just to create parts; it is to perfect them and harmonize them with everything else, so one thing flows into the next . . . and ends with good scores.

Additional Learning References

Teaching the Shot Sequence by Steve Ruis (AFm, Vol 12, No 5)
Your Personal Shot Sequence by Tom Dorigatti (AFm, Vol 14, No 4 & 5)
Why You Need to teach a Shot Sequence by AER (AFm, Vol 15, No 6)

Left to its own devices, the bow rebounds out of the bow hand, is caught by the sling, and rolls over because the bow arm is being held up. Doing anything else muddies the feedback that this action provides.
(Photo Courtesy of Andy Macdonald)

Still More on Coaching Archery

Chapter 10
Why the Bow Hand Release
is a Bad Idea

I was reading a recent issue of *Bogensport Magazin* and an article on Olympic Recurve shooting technique by Günter Kuhr caught my eye. In that article he brought up the "bow hand release." The caption to the illustrative photo was "Upon release of the string the bow hand snaps down so that the bow can swing free." I hope to explain why this is a nonsensical thing to do in this chapter.

Hiistory of the Bow Hand Release

The bow hand release has been around at least 500 years but for most of that time it was a simple avoidance of bow shock. We were shooting traditional bows with firm bow hands and the residual vibration from many shots was debilitating, so the practice came to be to "stop squeezing the bow just after string's release," so that vibration wouldn't be transmitted to the archer. Thus, the "bow hand release" was born.

The practice died out in the recurve era as the bows became heavier and more efficient, and less vibration was involved. Modern bows have vibration-dampening accessories to lessen the amount that could be transferred to the archer even further.

The modern version of the bow hand release is to snap the bow wrist down upon release of the string. Why this is done is somewhat mysterious, which is why you can read nonsensical things like Herr Kuhr's assertion "so that the bow can swing free." All of this takes place after the shot is gone (you hope) so the advantage of allowing the bow to "swing free" is a mystery.

Why This "Bow Hand Release" Makes No Sense

Obviously if this release is done inconsistently, it can inject error into shots. But, as mentioned, it should happen after the arrow is gone so it should have no effect on the shot. Consider that when the string is loosed, the archer moves from the full-draw-state in which much of the weight of the bow is being held up with the draw arm to the post loose state where the entire weight is borne by the bow arm alone. Since it only takes about 0.015 s for the arrow to leave the string and become freely flying, the bow cannot move much in that short of a time, but almost everybody remembers working through a bout of "dropping your bow arm" when we were beginners. Some effort needs to be made to accept that greater load on the bow arm to avoid a greater vertical spread in one's groups.

So, while the archer is accepting the greater load on his bow arm, he then snaps his bow wrist down. At that time the bow has jumped out to be caught in the archer's sling, so a roughly six-pound weight is "in hand" when this is done. This is a recipe for a repetitive stress injury if there ever was one. And what is the benefit? Since the arrow is already gone, how can that possibly help the shot? There is no benefit that I can see.

The action of snapping the wrist down replaces the natural action of the bow pulling the wrist down as the bow rolls. If one allows the followthrough to just happen, rather than trying to guide it into a channel, the followthrough can be observed by the archer and learned from. If the followthrough happens the same way every shot, it is an indication the archer is being consistent. If the motion of the bow changes, it can only be from forces injected by the archer, typically in the form of bow handle torque or plucking the string. Much of this is obscured if the bow wrist is swiftly dropped and that is too valuable information to just throw away.

What Should Happen Instead

Instead of a questionable bow hand activity, the bow hand and wrist should be as relaxed as possible. Being relaxed is repeatable, being tense is not. When the shot goes off, a form of recoil causes the bow to jump out of the relaxed bow hand to be caught by the archer's sling. The bow is balanced such that if allowed to fall freely through space it will rotate forward, so the bow does this and pulls the bow hand downward because the sling is attached to the hand. Since the bow arm is being held up, the bow completes its rotation while hanging from the sling. I use the completion of the bow's rotation as the signal that the shot is over: "The shot's not over until the bow takes a bow (the other 'bow')."

Conclusion

Any time we confuse "something that happens" with "something that we are to do," we create unnecessary complications and, well, trouble. The dropping of the bow hand at the end of a shot is something that happens because of the use of a sling and the position and configuration of the bow's mass. By interjecting "something to do" into this sequence, like a bow hand release movement, we muddy the information that can help us determine whether that was a good shot or, if not, what was done wrong.

Additional Learning References

Traditional Instinctive Shooting—The Bow Hand by Dan Quillian (AFm, Vol 4, No 2)
Bow Hand Loading and Stabilisation by Joe Tapley (AFm, Vol 13, No 2)
Understanding the Bow Hand by Larry Wise (AFm, Vol 12, No 3)

On Practice

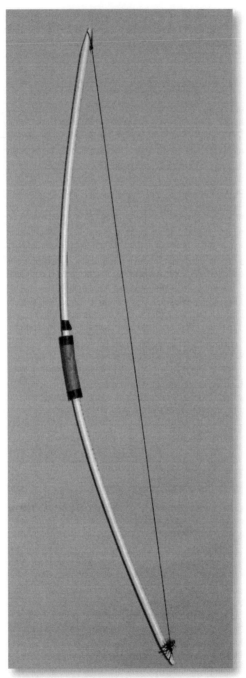

Can a bow made out of PVC pipe be used for serious practice?
(Photo Courtesy of Van Webster)

Still More on Coaching Archery

Chapter 11
Practice Tricks

I have written about practice extensively, including about practice planning (it doesn't have to be complicated, keep a notebook, etc.), how long to practice (short and intense is better than long and arduous), and how to structure practices (so many practice scoring rounds, so much equipment tuning, so much doing drills to improve form and execution, etc.). But there are some ways to make practice more effective and less boring and time consuming. Let's explore this topic. (They aren't really "tricks," but you have to admit the word makes for a catchy title!)

Speed It Up

When practicing at longer distances, instead of walking 70 m or whatever, there and back for each end of practice shooting, shorten the distance to save time. If you put a 60 cm target at 34.3 m it looks like a 122 cm target at 70 m. (It doesn't have to be exact.) Since your arrows are now two times wider to scale, you need to get at least a half shaft into a higher color to score the higher amount using this setup.

What you don't get is the proper angle of the shot, only having to hold your bow high enough to reach the shorter distance, so pin the target face as high as you can on the target butt. If you are a techno-weenie, you can figure out the proper launch angles and either elevate a target stand or pin the target face higher on the butt to simulate the 70 m bow angle at half that distance.

An Alternative Set up two target rounds and shoot two ends, one on either target, before fetching your arrows. This cuts the walking in half. The number of targets is only limited by the number of arrows you have. Be sure to allow at least 30s–60s of rest between "ends." You can also do this by shooting at one target but with two color-coded sets of arrows.

Routine Shakers for Practice Rounds
- Shoot 20-30 arrows to "warm up" before a Practice Round
- Shoot just two ends of "sighters" before a Practice Round
- Shoot just one end of "sighters" before a Practice Round
- Shoot no ends of "sighters" before a Practice Round, just start scoring.
- Only count the final half of a scoring end, doubling your score to have a score comparable to your others. This will help concentration and focus as you get deeper into an end, especially if you have been shooting three arrow ends all winter and now you have

five or six arrow ends.

Shoot With Your Eyes Closed for Score
This is probably best done at shorter distances, at least at first. Line up your shot as normal, then close your eyes and go through your normal finishing routine (expansion, etc.). If you find your arrows consistently drifting to the left or right, what does that tell you? Drifting up or down?

Mix It Up
Shoot the "other guy's" target faces. If you generally shoot FITA/WA target faces (the many colored ones), shoot the NFAA's targets instead or vice-versa. Note that they are scored differently and are often shot at different distances. Variety is the spice of life. You may find spots in your shot sequence when you tend to hang up when you do this. These are the same places you will hang up when experiencing difficulties shooting the target faces you think of as "normal."

Aiming Off Practice
Try Reverse Scoring Shoot ends with reverse scoring, *e.g.* the 1-ring is worth 10, the 2-ring nine, etc. Pick a line, *e.g.* "from 11 o'clock to the center of the target," and try to shoot arrows on that line that score well. Change the "scoring line" from end to end.

Mis-Set Your Sight to Practice Aiming Off On a windless day, deliberately mis-set your sight and then figure out how to shoot in the middle by "aiming off." Start at shorter distances and smaller mis-sets until you get the knack of it. After shooting for a while holding high-left, for example, change your mis-set so you will need to aim high-right or low-right. Mix it up. Make it your challenge to be "in the center" with the fewest misses possible (the lowest number of arrows shot to tell you how to aim off is one).

The Imaginary Green Dot Technique Place a "different" color-aiming dot elsewhere on the target (green is a good color as few targets have any green on them). Make it approximately the size of the highest scoring ring. (Measure it and then go shopping for press-on dots of that size.) Shoot at the green dot for several practices, moving the dot (or placing a new one if it gets shot up) each time. Then try your hand at imagining the green dot to be in a particular place (five o'clock in the blue) and aim at it and shoot. How do your groups shot at an imaginary dot compare with your groups shot at a real dot? *Note* Some archers can make this work, others cannot. If you can, you can create an imaginary aiming dot anywhere you want on a target. The key is to be able to fix it in place. Since, in competition, the arrows will be landing in target center, rather than the green dot, you won't have a group of arrows to shoot at. So, if you can make this work, combine the "Imaginary Green Dot" procedure with mis-setting your sight so you can get used to it the way it will be used. A key point is having a phrase like "five o'clock in the blue" to use to fix the location of your imaginary dot.

Test Your Endurance
If you think you are in good "shooting shape," grab another bow with 5-10 pounds of extra draw weight and shoot a "mock end" with that bow before shooting a regular end with your bow during a practice round. A "mock end" involves you going through your normal routine, but every "shot" ends in a letdown. Don't start with a lot of extra weight; try it first with your bow (effectively making a six-arrow end into a twelve-arrow end, or a five-arrow

end into a ten arrow end). *Note* A fun way to do this is make a "pipe bow" with the desired poundage (*see reference below*).

Another variation of this drill is "Double Draws." For each arrow of a practice end, let down from full draw to brace (compound) or setup position (recurve) and then go right back up for the actual shot.

You may need multi-spot targets for this variant: shoot two arrows in a practice round in place of each one. You only get to count the second arrow. If you are outdoors, you may have to mark your shafts if shooting at a single face, or pin up two faces, one for the first arrows, one for the second arrows. Track the hit points and/or scores on both sets. While this is a conditioning drill, it will also point up flaws in your shooting consistency. For example, if your second arrows (the scoring ones) group better than the first, you are not as fully engaged with your first arrows as you are your second (you want to be mentally fully engaged in all arrows shot, a major criterion for being consistent). Obviously, if your shots deeper into such an end don't score as well as the earlier ones, your conditioning is suspect.

Practice "Running Out of Time" Shots

Have a friend or shooting partner count down a time clock for you after you reach full draw (or even before). Your friend is creating time pressure for you to experience and learn to deal with. So, you hit full draw and they say "... four ... three ... two," etc. and your job is to get the shot off before the whistle. If they start counting before the bow is raised, they start at 8 seconds (or 9, or 10—mix it up). You may be surprised at how anxious you feel in this situation. (Also proving, again, that all pressure is self-induced.) If you do feel anxiety in this practice drill, imagine what will happen when you are in competition and have to get a shot off quickly. This drill is designed to take the edge off of that situation and allow you the time to devise a strategy for when it does happen.

Release shooters have special considerations as they cannot just relax their fingers to get the arrow off.

This form of practice needs to be done in moderation because while you are "under pressure" it is far easier to burn in bad habits.

Extending This Practice Mode Analyze your shot to see if there are other situations that create anxiety in you (or your archer if you are a coach). Devise ways to simulate these situations in practice and do that. Talk with others about what they do when something like that occurs to them.

Additional Learning References

Sight Change Drills by Bob Ryder (AFm, Vol 17, No 6)
The Elements of Good Practice by AER (AFm, Vol 15, No 3)
Tournament Site Practice by Larry Wise (AFm, Vol 17, No 5)
Do You Practice with a Plan? by Tom Dorigatti (AFm, Vol 13, No 3)
Preparing to Perform by Steve Ruis (AFm, Vol 13, No 2)
Pipe Bows as Practice Bows by Van Webster (AFm, Vol 12, No 3)

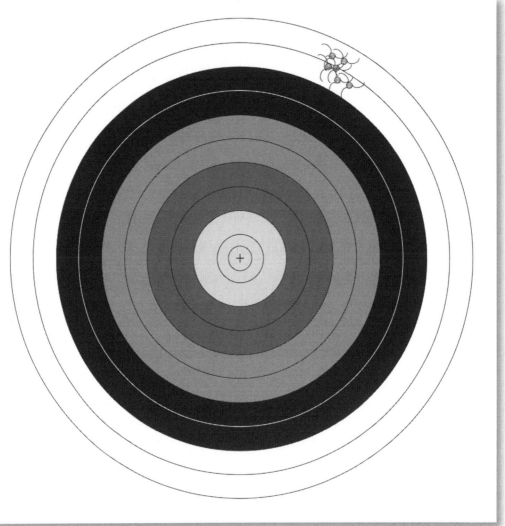

A Good group? Yep! But what are you telling your subconscious mind? Are you telling yourself that groups in the white are something you are comfortable with? Move that group on center and tell yourself that you "live in the center."

Still More on Coaching Archery

Chapter 12
Why You Should Always
Center Your Groups

I see it all the time. An archer is shooting good groups in practice but they aren't centered on the target. I am here to tell you that you should always center your groups. Here's why.

A Cautionary Caveat

Having had range maintenance duties for many years, I know that it is important that target faces be placed "off center" or at least in various positions so that the butts wear evenly. If you always place the target face in the same spot and always "center your groups" you will make a soft spot in that place and lessen the lifespan of the target. Think while you are pinning up target faces! Move them around and spread the wear and tear on the target butt.

The Physical Benefits

If you adjust your sight so your groups are always centered on the target face, you can use decimal scoring of your arrows in practice to tell you how tight your groups are. Decimal scoring is giving a score to each arrow that includes tenths of points. An arrow just into the next higher scoring ring, say a 4-ring, might get a score of 4.1. Another arrow just outside of the 5-ring might get a score of 4.9. You add one tenth of a point for each tenth of the distance between rings. An arrow in the middle of the 4-ring would be given a 4.5. If you want more information, you can also record the clock position with that score. An example is 4.5/11. This arrow hit halfway through the 4-ring at 11 o'clock.

By centering your groups on the target center, your average decimal score is an indicator of your group size. An average of 4.5 is superior to 4.1. Tracking this from practice to practice tells you whether your groups are getting smaller over time . . . or not.

If you don't center your groups on the target face, you could have a tight group on the outer edge of the target face and the scores would say very little about your group size (*see illustration left*). Centered that group would probably score 59 or 60 which would tell you a lot about it and would feel substantially different.

The Psychological Benefits

If the above benefit were the only one, it might not be worth doing. But in this case the mental benefits are far greater than the physical ones!

For example, consider the impact on your self-image if, say on the NFAA 5-spot indoor target, your last 200 shots were in the white spot. How confident would you be that you could put shot 201 into the white also? Probably pretty high. This does not mean that shot 201 is guaranteed to go into the spot, just that it has a very high likelihood of doing so.

Mental Coach Lanny Bassham has said it over and over again: "your self-image determines your performance." And your self-image is based upon prior behavior. If you typically lied, cheated, and stole from other people, you wouldn't be shocked if you just did it again. On the other hand, if your self-image is that of someone who never lied, or stole anything, or cheated anyone, it would probably shock you if anyone would even suggest doing those things.

This is not just a "practice makes perfect" kind of thing. It is an actual feeling of "who we are" that we all have. If you have been an archer for any length of time, you will probably have had this experience (which no one shares with others when it happens to them, unless they've been clued in ahead of time): you were shooting arrows and got into a streak in which you felt like you couldn't miss. You were shooting "lights out" and you were accumulating a score higher than anything you have ever shot. And then you missed . . . and you felt relief. What the heck? What's wrong with me, that I would feel good about missing?

What you were feeling was called your *comfort zone*. You were shooting a score that put you in with the "big boys (or girls)" and you weren't one of them, you just weren't. So, when you missed, you took it as evidence that you were back to performing like you expected to from your own self-image.

Your comfort zone has a bottom to it. If you are shooting very poorly, you can feel disappointment and even anger that you are doing so poorly and mentally grab yourself by the scruff of the neck, give yourself a good shake, and start shooting better.

The problem with your comfort zones is they are boxes that confine your performances. If you want to be a consistent, accurate archer, you have to make a transition from someone who misses a lot (all beginners) to someone who misses rarely. And you are hard to convince. You need to see a lot of arrows going into the center to convince yourself that you are someone who shoots high scores. (Can you see where I am going?)

Your subconscious mind cannot tell the difference between an arrow shot in practice and one shot in competition. If you shoot a bunch of arrows in a face's outer rings and you do that often, then you are training your self-image that shooting arrows in the outer rings is normal for you, part of your self-image and your scoring comfort zone.

So, don't do it! Center your groups. Allow your subconscious mind to get an honest look at your abilities. No amount of positive thinking drills ("I think I can, I think I can, . . .") will work if you contradict them by shooting groups off center. If you don't care where the arrows land take the target face down!

"Whether you think you can or you think you can't . . . you are right." Henry Ford

The key point here is the thinking that counts isn't conscious thinking and it sure isn't lying to yourself (saying "yes" when you know the answer should be "no").

Additional Learning References

Do You Expect to Win? by Steve Ruis (AFm, Vol 14, No 6)
Scorecard Analysis in Archery by Ava McDowell (AFm, Vol 9, No 2)
A 'Simple Tech' Approach to Group Tuning by Steve Ruis (AFm, Vol 14, No 4)

A release aid—how far do you think you could shoot one?

Still More on Coaching Archery

Chapter 13
A Practice Prescription Case Study:
After a Longish Layoff

I got the following letter from one of my compound students:

"The lessons last year were great. I didn't do any archery during the winter, seemed every other day I was doing snow. Also got a late start this year and have been out only five times. I have a strange problem that concerns me. Maybe you've seen it.

"I was using the back tension release last year from August until mid-October. Seemed to be getting the hang of it going out several times a week. Every once in a while I'd let the bow down about an inch, something you noticed I was doing and called it "vacillating." (*I think rather collapsing or creeping*. SR) When I would do it with the back tension release, off went the arrow. I don't think this is safe and never want an arrow going off without me doing it, not to mention losing several arrows. I stopped using it and went back to the Carter *Insatiable* thumb trigger release I've been using for years. Couple trips after going back to it, for some reason I let go of the release at full draw instead of pressing the button. It hit me in the bow hand knuckle and gave me a decent cut, luckily not too bad though. I made one more trip out before ending for the season with no problems.

"Earlier this week, only my fifth time out this season, I was shooting with the Carter *Insatiable* and just before pressing the trigger, I let go of the release. It hit the riser then went back over my right shoulder about 25 feet behind me. Couldn't find the arrow even with the white wraps I put on. I was very lucky it didn't hit my bow hand or come back and hit me. The rest of my outing all I could think about was making sure not to somehow let go of the release. I tried to figure how or why I did what I did but could only think it's some muscle memory of the back tension release I was using last year. Maybe when I'm relaxing my bow hand I relax my release hand as well. Regardless, It's not safe and I won't keep using that release. I have a trigger release with the wrist strap I'll use.

"Have you ever heard of this happening? Do you think I can wrap a wrist sling around the Carter *Insatiable* to make sure I don't let it go?

"I don't think this is a medical condition as I do other activities where I need to hold things and I don't drop things. I've never had this problem except for these two times I've described.

Thanks"

What's Happening?

What do you think happened here? Take a moment or two to come up with a diagnosis before reading farther. Then compare your "read" with mine.

Here's My Response

Let go of your release aid? Heck, I've done that myself.

It is always prudent, especially when you were learning something new when you started the layoff, to be very deliberate when restarting, even to the point of talking yourself through your shot sequence for several shots. Always (always, always) review what you were working on before starting up again (you wrote it down in your notebook, no?). If you don't do this you'll get a mishmash of your old style with elements of the new mixed in … uh, randomly or at least unpredictably.

It is also a very good idea to crank the bow down, too, if you can. Your archery muscles haven't been worked in quite a while, so give them a chance to get back up to speed.

Triggerless releases in particular require you to be very deliberate and move the release away from a position where it might go off before you begin the letdown. If it has a safety, reset it before you begin the letdown. It is very easy to rotate your hand the wrong way when it is moving forward rather than backward, so you must be very deliberate. If you are doing a letdown, be sure to aim at the ground in front of you (outdoors) or the target (indoors) while executing the letdown as mis-launches happen, even to the best of us. As an aside, I think it is a good idea to practice letdowns from time to time. It is something I teach all of my students.

Having shot one of my own release aids over 25 yards (it went farther than the arrow!) I do have some experience here and I think a good idea is to use a wrist lanyard on the release (at least until you have retrained). There used to be holes in the release aids for these (if not, you can tie one on). The lanyard got looped around your wrist (like a wrist sling) so that the release hung just and inch or two outside of its normal position. Coach Frank Pearson even taught that to train for a really relaxed release hand you should drop your release after the string goes (on a lanyard, of course).

Starting up after a long layoff can include all kinds of surprises which is why you want to double check your equipment, turn down the draw weight (or swap in a lighter pair of limbs if a recurve bow is being used or even use a lighter weight bow at first), and review what you were doing when you started your layoff. Such layoffs can be long (months) or just a few weeks. If you take them casually, you may be doing damage to your learned form and execution or even yourself, as was almost the case here.

Additional Learning References

Practice Prescription, Part 1 **Even More on Coaching Archery** (WAF, 2013)
Practice Prescription, Part 2 **Even More on Coaching Archery** (WAF, 2013)

The Anatomy of a Letdown

As mentioned I teach beginners how to do a letdown of a shot. This is a purely safety precaution. What we want to avoid are accidental loosings.

In General The procedure is roughly the same indoors and out with one major exception. The procedure is to deliberately return the bow to brace position by letting the bow pull the string back into place. Indoors this is done while aiming solidly at the target butt. Outdoors this is done by aiming at the ground close up.

The purpose of aiming at the ground outdoors is two fold: safety and in target archery there is a rule in one organization that an arrow shot three meters or less (about 10 feet) does not count as a shot arrow, so if you have an accidental loose why have it counted as a scored arrow or why spend time looking for the arrow behind the target?

Indoors the floors are hard enough that if you aim at the floor in a similar fashion that arrow will ricochet somewhere and will probably be destroyed in the process, hence the procedure to keep the arrow pointed at something that can receive it safely (*Hint* your target butt).

The Special Case of Compound Archers The importance of practicing doing a letdown is clearly seen when compound archers do it the first time. The force draw curve is steep . . . *both ways* . . . and one must brace oneself for the return trip. Otherwise the bow will jerk the string out of the archer's hand. The feeling of pulling the string to full draw is quite different from the bow pulling the string back.

The Special Case of Release Shooters If you shoot with a release aid, the first step must be to deactivate your release aid. If your finger was on the trigger, take it off. If you were using a triggerless release with a safety, re-engage the safety. If you were using a rotary triggerless release without a safety, rotate the release aid backward so it won't be in a critical position during the letdown.

This can't be practice surely; practice is supposed to be fun, but. . . .
(Photo Courtesy of Andy Macdonald)

Still More on Coaching Archery

Chapter 14
Enjoying Practice

You will not succeed without practice, a lot of practice.
You will not do a lot of practice unless you enjoy it. Anonymous

If you have never heard this before, you are a pretty rare bird. This sounds true, does it not? It sounds simple, too, right? But it is not. What does the author mean by "enjoy?" Does this mean that practice needs to be "fun?" I know what *I* mean by this: I mean that the linkage between now (at the beginning of a practice session) and previous practice sessions is a positive one and not a negative one. It does not mean that you have to feel joy as you practice, flooding your brain with endorphins and feeling the equivalent of a "runner's high." It also doesn't mean you won't, just that it isn't required.

Consider mountain climbers. If you have read any accounts of significant climbs (K2, Everest, etc.) you'll have read a long list of problems and woes. Climbing a really high mountain is expensive, it requires a great deal of training and preparation, and the actual climb is anything but fun: it can involve frost bite, difficulty breathing, leg cramps, being unable to sleep, ferocious storms, and accounts of members of one's party dying from falls, anoxia, and disease. Any sane person having experienced this would say "never again, I must have been crazy." Yet people do this over and over. For "fun," we say.

Archery practice, while being far less dramatic than extreme mountain climbing, has elements in common with it. It is something no one else is requiring you or paying you to do. You have volunteered to do it. And, on the surface it doesn't seem like a "fun activity," certainly not the 435th repetition of it. So, where does the "enjoyment" come from?

Martial artists talk about practice with phrases like "eating bitter," *e.g.* if you want to be really good, you have to "eat bitter" in practice. In other words, you have to work so hard in practice, with so little reward, that it leaves a bitter taste in your mouth. Football players and bodybuilders talk about "paying the price" in workouts.

It is starting to sound like the introductory statement is one of those assertions that sound true but are illusory, but I feel it really is true. The problem lies in the use of overworked words like "enjoy."

Real Practice

The real situation is this. You do not have a supervisor to organize or judge your work. You have to manage yourself. So, when the idea of practice comes into your head, there is a connection to your previous practice session and weaker echoes to sessions before that. If those connections don't help motivate you to engage in further practice, you are likelier to beg off, skip, or skimp on the session in hand. After all, the only person you have to convince to slack off is yourself. As an aside, this is one of the advantages of having a training partner. It is easier for you to just talk yourself out of practicing (or quitting early, or . . .) than talking yourself and a training partner out of it.

The opening quotation indicates that some joy must be associated with those previous practice sessions or keeping going is going to be a slog, a dreary task that you'd rather not do. But joy isn't just a simple sensation of pleasure. Like the mountain climbers, it can come from a sense of accomplishment, doing something difficult and doing it well, or any number of other things. So, how do you know you did anything particularly well in your last practice? Do you just depend on memory and emotions? I think you had better not.

Your practice has to mean something. If you are "just flinging arrows" how can you evaluate that? This is where practice planning comes into play. If your last practice had a short list of things to accomplish associated with it (ah, there's the list in your notebook) and next to each of those items is a check mark indicating the successful completion of those tasks, then that practice was satisfying at a bare minimum. Jack Nicklaus, the Hall of Fame golfer, was famous for saying about practice "Achieve, then leave." He was not one to go to the practice range and bang balls for no reason. And if you do not have a list of things to accomplish, how will you know you accomplished anything? Of course, I prefer written lists as they provide a record that doesn't suffer from faulty memory.

By taking the time to plan your practices, you automatically have a mechanism to evaluate what you did. If you, say, want to tune your new arrows so that they bare shaft well out to 50m, either that gets done or it does not. If it doesn't, it is not an occasion to berate yourself, it may just be you need more time to get it right, so that goal gets carried over to your next practice session. If you do get it done, you get a check mark. Another task done satisfactorily.

The Thousand Arrow Challenge

A few Olympic recurve archers have taken the 1000 Arrow Challenge. The task is to shoot 1000 practice arrows in one day. This is not done lightly. It requires the arrows be shot properly. (Why would you practice doing it wrong?) It requires preparation. It is done blank bale and can take up most of the daylight hours of a summer day. It helps if someone else pulls your arrows. After the first few hundred shots, it can become a boring, almost stultifying, task. After the half way mark, you may start questioning why you thought this might be a good idea. Toward the end, the muscles in your back may be screaming for relief.

So, where's the joy in this? Like the mountain climbers, there is very little direct pleasure you can take out of this task. But there is a great deal of satisfaction in meeting such a challenge. After accomplishing such a feat, you will have a hard time telling yourself that something you need to do is "too hard" or "beyond your abilities."

Summary

There may be direct pleasure experienced during practice, for example, the feeling you get when your body supports what you want to do and performs really well. More often, though, practice consists of routine tasks, such as drills, equipment tuning, etc. that don't provide direct pleasure, but if placed in an overall plan can give satisfaction in the form of successfully accomplished tasks.

So, do you have to enjoy practice? If you do not, you are unlikely to go far. But with some planning and organization, you can create a chain of successful practices that provide the pleasures of accomplishment that will keep you going through thick and thin.

Additional Learning References

Do You Practice with a Plan? by Tom Dorigatti (AFm, Vol 13, No 3)
Preparing to Perform by Steve Ruis (AFm, Vol 13, No 2)
Finding the Fun in Archery Again by Lorretta Sinclair (AFm, Vol 13, No 2)
Are You Losing Interest in Archery? by Colin Remmer (AFm, Vol 10, No 4)
Developing Your Edge by Tim Scronce (AFm, Vol 8, No 2)

On Equipment

Arrow Overhang: how far is too far?

Still More on Coaching Archery

Chapter 15
Arrow Overhang—
How Much Is Too Much?

If you have been around archery for any time, you have probably noticed that some archers' arrows stick out from their bows at full draw more than others. Is there an amount of arrow overhanging the rest that is too much? I will give you a clue: you won't often see elite archers with their arrows sticking out past the back of the riser. You may, especially indoors where archers are using the fattest possible shafts, which are therefore the stiffest possible shafts and have to be shot full length to offset some of that stiffness, but you will not see this outdoors.

Clearly this is a complicated topic, so let's look at it in some detail.

Arrow Overhang—Yes!

There are instances in which a fair amount of arrow overhang is a good thing. Start with the fact that arrows that are "too short" are dangerous. They can be pulled off of the back of the arrow rest with the point falling onto the back of the archer's bow hand. If the arrow is accidentally loosed, the outcome is a serious accident. So, archers whose draw lengths are not quite consistent need a fair bit of overhang. This is why program arrows for beginning archers are guaranteed to be "too long." We aren't worried about arrow dynamics so much but about beginning archery safely.

The same is true for youths, even if they are somewhat expert as archers. Because they are young, they are still growing. For each one inch they grow taller, their draw length goes up by one half of an inch. If parents and coaches don't pay enough attention, a young archer can grow out of their arrows in as little as a summer.

In addition, as youths grow, they get stronger and often are then capable of a little more draw weight. A longer draw length and a higher draw weight require stiffer arrows. Consequently when I fit "still growing" archers for arrows, I generally fit them with arrows 2-3 spine groups stiffer and cut them 2-3 inches "too long" to balance that out. Then if the archer's draw length picks up an inch, I can cut an inch off of his arrows and we are back to having well-spined arrows, easy peasy.

Arrow Overhang—No (Well, Maybe)!

Once an archer has his full growth or steady form so that his draw length and weight are settled, is there any advantage or disadvantage to having a large overhang? The answer is "probably no advantage" and perhaps even a disadvantage.

Let me use one of my student's arrows as an example. The shaft is an Easton ACE (Spine 0.470, length 31.5 inches) and it hangs over the rest about two inches longer than it needs to be. If we were to go with a 570 ACE (two spine groups weaker) and cut it two inches shorter, we would benefit in a number of ways. For one, we would lose two inches of the shaft, which weighs 6.3 gr/in, so there is 12.6 grains less arrow weight. Also the 470s weigh more (6.8 grains per inch), so the 570s would weigh 0.5 gr/in x 29.5 in = 14.75 gr less for a total weight reduction of 27.4 gr.

This archer was using a 110-gr point. Now he can have quite the same FOC (front-of-center balance) with a 100-gr point, making the total weight reduction 37.4 gr.

This is more than 10% of the total weight of the arrow and will significantly improve arrow speed, which improves cast and time-of-flight, which will in turn allow the archer a more level posture at longer shooting distances and less trouble from the wind.

So, what do you think? Worth doing?

The elites think so, as they have all done this.

So, What Should I Do?

If you have a considerable amount of arrow hanging out the back of your bow, should you change arrows? Well, maybe. If you are still growing, no. If you are still developing your archery form, no. If you just bought new arrows? This is tough. If you just paid a lot of money for new arrows, even if you could sell them on the secondary market, you may take a financial hit, so this is something you might wait to do when you need new arrows the next time.

How Do I Do Fit Arrows to the Correct Length?

If you are curious, you need to learn how to do this yourself.

The Background First, find an arrow manufacturer's spine chart (*see p. 84 for an example*). You can find them online and in archery catalogs. Any manufacturer will do. Look at how they are set up. We inherited this chart design from the early twentieth century arrow manufacturers (first wood, then aluminum). Basically across the top you have column labels corresponding to draw lengths and down the side you have row labels corresponding to draw weights.

The draw lengths, more properly "arrow lengths," across the top are in one-inch increments. In the early days, draw length wasn't measured the same as we do now and the distance was defined as being from the string (bottom of the nock's groove) to where the arrow sat on the shelf or archer's knuckle (at full draw). Today we call this the True Draw Length. But archers who bought arrows at those lengths had problems pulling the arrows off of their resting points, so a new definition was created "the AMO Draw Length" as an industry standard. (The Archery Merchants and Manufacturers Association (AMO) closed its doors and reopened them as the Archery Trade Association (ATA), so you may hear of this referred to as the ATA Draw Length.) The AMO Draw Length was defined to be the True Draw Length plus 1¾ inches. The "extra" length needed to overhang the rest was added in. (The "1¾ inches" was a rough average of the distance from the arrow rest to the back of the bow because measuring draw length all the way to the back of the bow was one traditional way of measuring draw length.)

So AMO Draw Length and Arrow Length should be about the same. You want a little arrow hanging over the rest, but not a lot.

Look at the spine chart. In the boxes on the intersections of the various draw lengths and draw weights you will find that manufacturer's spine recommendation. And if you focus on one particular shaft/spine, you will find it listed on a forty-five degree angle (bottom left to top right) through the chart. In fact all or almost all of them can be found "on the diagonal" of the chart. Because the spine chart was so successful in helping people find the right arrows, no manufacturer wanted to change the setup, so every new manufacturer built their arrows so they would form the same pattern.

Because of this, there is a rule of thumb: for every five pounds you want to change draw weight (up or down), the shaft has to change one inch in length to accommodate this change. There is only so much you can chop off of an arrow shaft, so a number of different shafts with different spines have to be made, but you can find manufacturers that cover from 35-70 pounds of draw with just three shafts. Be careful, though; the spine adjustments are made by cutting the shafts. If your draw length is really long or short, you can be misled a great deal.

All of the arrows that have approximately the same spine are called a spine group (and they sit in one of the little boxes in the chart).

The Procedure Basically, if you have an arrow that is performing well, all you need is the same arrow from the same manufacturer, only one spine group less stiff (move one box to the left from where you are on the chart) which you then cut off one inch shorter. If you are two inches too long, move two boxes, cut off two inches. If three inches, move three boxes, cut three inches.

Anytime I change to a new shaft I always do so cautiously. I don't want to just "trust the charts." I deliberately cut the new shafts long and then bare shaft test them. I then cut small increments off of a test set (three fletched, two bare) until the bare shaft test is exactly as I want it and only then cut the rest.

I do this because arrows cut too long can be corrected; arrows cut too short can only be sold.

Additional Learning References

On Arrows by Rick McKinney (AFm, Vol 11, No 1)
Precision Arrow Building—Have We Been Doing It Wrong? by Curtis Horton (AFm, Vol 8, No 5)
Arrow Selection by Vittorio Frangilli (AFm, Vol 6, No 1),
also in **The Heretic Archer** by Vittorio and Michele Frangilli
The Art of Making Perfect Arrows by Pedro Serrheiro (AFm, Vol 3, No 5)

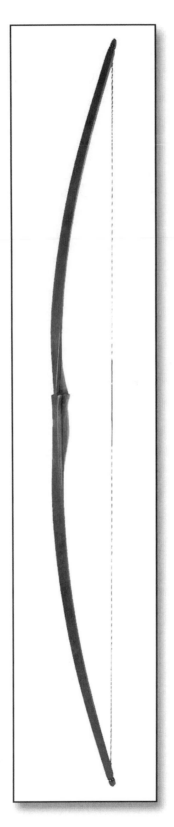

The Bearpaw Twin Bow

Still More on Coaching Archery

Chapter 16
The Bearpaw Twin Bow:
A Coach's Perspective

One of the difficulties encountered in coaching young beginners is how to introduce them to traditional archery. We generally start kids on light drawing recurve bows and some on compound bows. The compound bow starts are limited to kids who can hold the considerably heavier compound bows. The introduction of the *Genesis* compound solved many of the problems of starting beginners on a compound bow, but there are tradeoffs. The "zero letoff" feature creates a bow without a fixed draw length which is absolutely necessary for classes of kids using the same bows over and over, but the loss of letoff is the loss of what makes compound bows special. Then there is the sheer mass of compound bows. They are too heavy for a considerable fraction of kids. This is why the general starting point is with a light drawing, light-in-weight, recurve bow. (They are cheaper, too.)

In traditional archery there are longbows and recurves being shot, so the recurve bows that kids start with puts them on the path to traditional archery. At the same time, the addition of sights and stabilizers and clickers takes them off of that path. The question is how to show beginners what traditional archery is like by having them do something different. Shooting the same recurve bows they were shooting isn't exactly different. The solution is introducing them to longbows. The problem is there are very few that are suitable.

In California, a rather eminent bowyer made us quite a few 15# longbows for our classes. He did so at a price that surely couldn't have made him any money on the deal, but each of us gives back to the sport in our own way. That was then and this is now. The kind of bow I think we are looking for is 20# of draw or less, with laminated limbs (for safety and durability) and an arrow shelf (so as to not have to deal with shooting off the hand). If you look around, you will find almost none of these. What we did find is the Bearpaw *Twin Bow*, which we think makes an excellent bow for coaches to introduce traditional longbow shooting to students. It can be shot both left- and right-handed by most kids and adults and comes in draw weights as low as 20#.

Because of the highlighting of traditional archery in movies like *The Hunger Games* and myriad others, quite a number of other suitable youth longbows are now being made available, to which we say "Hallelujah!"

The Bearpaw Twin Bow

Bearpaw is a German company with quite a large catalog (you can see it here: https://shop.bearpaw-products.com/). The *Twin Bow* is an American flat bow design. The finish was "fair" in that there were a few rough spots that needed touching up either with a fine round file (in the limb tip notches) or sandpaper (elsewhere). The finish is quite dull, so don't expect the same as you would get from custom bowyer. We put a couple of coats of paste wax on the bow, just for waterproofing purposes. The bow comes with a nice Dacron Flemish twist bowstring, a single shelf pad (see photos) and a clamp-on brass nock locator. We expected to get two shelf pads for a bow with two shelves, but. . . .

The two "shelves" are barely that, but one cannot expect a deep cut sight window on a bow being shot both ways. We intend to do a little experimenting with this bow; one of the things we will try is to cut the shelves, not so much in, but sharper, so they hold the arrow better. With the shelves rounded as they are (*see photos*), you must shoot off of the shelf and a bit of knuckle to keep the arrow in place. But for this review the bow was shot as supplied.

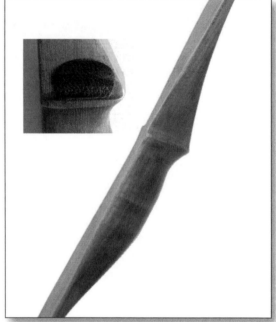

The Test To get an impression of whether this 20# bow could perform at all, I took it to the 2014 Bowman Round shoot at the Wheaton Rifle Club archery range. The Bowman Round was first developed by the United Bowmen of Philadelphia (if not the oldest archery club in existence in the United States, one of them). This round was first shot in the early-to-mid 1800s. It consists of 14 ends of six arrows shot at the 122 cm FITA target at 80 yards with traditional scoring (9, 7, 5, 3, 1). I shot this round the previous year (2013) with my #1 bow, made for me by Brian Luke. It is an Osage Orange self bow, 72″, 35# @ 32″ of draw.

I found some wooden arrows in my stash that seemed to fly quite well (no serious tuning was done as this was to just get an impression) and tied on nocking point locators and I was off to the shooting line. Interestingly enough, even though the Bearpaw bow as quite a bit lighter in draw, the points of aim for the distance were quite similar. This, we believe, is the advantage of fiberglass-reinforced limbs over self bows: they are more resilient and hence you get more arrow speed per pound of draw.

The *Twin Bow* was smooth to draw all the way back to my 32″ draw. Stacking seemed minimal. All-in-all, it was fun to shoot and had no trouble reaching the 80-yard target. My score was less than the previous year but I don't exactly practice a whole lot either.

Conclusions

Make no mistake, this is not a competition bow *per se*. We do think, though, it is a perfect starter bow for coaches who want to introduce traditional archery to teenagers and adults. Whether your student is right- or left-handed, they can shoot this bow. The draw weight is low enough that almost any beginner can get arrows to fly. We do recommend that you leave wooden arrows until later (although we do show off some pretty ones as the sheer beauty of the equipment is part of the allure of traditional archery). We suggest you stick to aluminum arrows until your students are quite proficient.

We haven't had this bow for long but the laminated limbs and simple design lead us to believe that it will hold up for quite some time (self bows tend to break way more often). We will be exploring reshaping the arrow shelves (without cutting into the handle any deeper) to see if they can be made to hold the arrows without an assist from the bow hand.

Because coaches often have to schlep equipment around from place to place, the only think that could have made this bow any better is if it were a two piece takedown model, but we are not holding our breath. There are plenty of wonders available in the form of traditional longbows and recurves, but for these purposes, having a low price tag is a key positive factor. There is no reason that students who take to traditional longbow shooting should not buy this bow as their first.

Bearpaw *Twin Bow*
Bow Length 68″
Draw Weights 20#, 25#, 30#, 35#
Brace Height 6¾″
Laminated limbs

Additional Learning References
So You Want to Try Traditional? by Brian J. Luke (AFm, Vol 13, No 5)
Consider the Longbow by Brian J. Luke (AFm, Vol 5, No 5)
Traditional Equipment by Dan Quillian (AFm, Vol 4, No 6)
Bowstrings, Fistmeles, and Traditional Bows by Dan Quillian (AFm, Vol 3, No 6)
What is Traditional Archery? by T.J. Conrads (AFm, Vol 1, No 2)

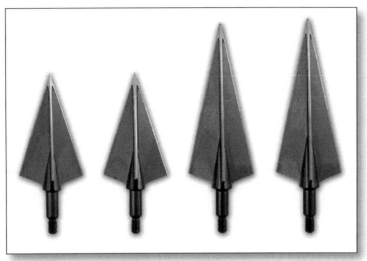

They look like they could fly, don't they?

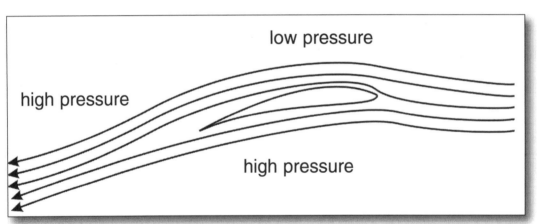

The way airplane wings work is their asymmetrical shape requires air to flow a longer distance over the top than the bottom of the wing. This creates a high air pressure under the wing and a low air pressure above it, the difference in the two air "pushes" is the "lift" that gets the plane off of he ground. This is exaggerated by tilting the wings at takeoff and minimized by leveling them when at the desired elevation.

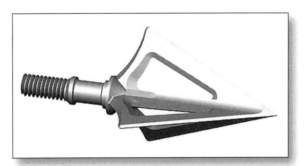

And how well do you think a plane wll fly if you punch big holes in the wings? Uh, huh.

Chapter 17
The Broadhead Planing Effect: Fact or BS?

Fact or BS? Broadheads cause "planing" that redirects arrows off of line and therefore require extra stabilization in the form of larger vanes/feathers.

The Broadhead Planing Effect
The argument goes like this: the blades of the broadhead act like little airplane wings and, catching the air, cause it to "fly" off line.

Why I Don't Like This Argument Airplane wings have "lift" because they are curved in cross section (*see illustration left*). This creates two paths for the air to get past the wing, along the curved path on the top of the wing or upon the straighter path below the wing. Because the air takes more time on the longer path, the air molecules get spread out more, creating a zone of lower air pressure above the wing than below. Since pressure is force per unit of area there is a net force created by the difference between the higher pressure air below the wing and that lower pressure below it, causing the wing to move up.

The blades of a broadhead have no such curved shape. Instead they are flat and, in addition, they are perpendicular to the centerline of the shaft (if installed correctly) so they aren't even slanted to the air the arrow is flowing through (zero angle of attack, essentially). In addition, if there were a lift, it would either be doubled by the "wings" on the other side of the head (as it is on an airplane) or cancelled by (if the lift were in the opposite direction). In the second case there would be no "planing" effect and in the first it would merely increase or decrease the rotation of the arrow around its shaft center (depending on whether the blades were in the same orientation as the fletches or not). Neither of these effects would cause the shaft to go off line.

Where Did This "Explanation" Come From?
This is almost impossible to tell but I suspect it was from something like this . . . (I need some Ken Burns-ish story telling music here).

My hunch is that this discussion began back when hunters shot mostly with their fingers. This could be checked by looking to see if the "broadhead planing effect" was mentioned before the widespread use of release aids. I did this and found a mention (the term was "wind planing") in a book written in 1971, so this is fairly settled. Broadheads are, well, broad. Consequently they increase the frontal area of the arrow causing an even higher stack up of air in front (http://archeryreport.com/2010/02/arrowdynamics-ii-fun-broadheads/) than do field points. Broadheads are also longer than the field points one typically substitutes for them. Back when broadheads were much longer and much heavier than field points, this also changed the FOC balance of the arrow and the locations of the arrow's nodes. These factors indicate why the broadhead-tipped shafts would usually not hit in the exact same location as the field point-tipped shafts when shot from the same bow.

In addition, if the broadheads are not perfectly aligned with the center of the shaft, some wobble must occur when the fletches begin to rotate the shaft after the arrow comes off of the string. Any "wobble" due to the head or insert being the tiniest bit out of round (either due to its manufacture or installation) would lead to speculation as to why it would do that, and voilà, an "explanation" is born/guessed/imagined/figured/dreamed up.

Basically because the greater drag created by the broadhead contests to some extent with the drag of the fletches, especially in crosswinds, there is a need for "extra steerage" in the form of more effective fletching, but I think this has nothing to do with the blades of a broadhead acting like tiny airplane wings.

There is one situation in which the little "wings" will have an effect: in cross winds. The old two- and three-blade heads had quite a bit of side area to catch wind if a side wind were blowing. But trouble with the wind also affects the shaft (which has a much greater surface area from the side) and most hunting shots are made at relatively short distances with heavy arrows, etc., all of which reduce any such effects of the wind.

This topic has been discussed before but most of what I can find just passes on the bogus discussion from the past. Anybody out there got another idea of what's going on? Write about it, send it to me, and you will receive a check if we publish it in *Archery Focus* magazine.

Additional Learning References

Tuning Tips for Bowhunters by Jason Butler (AFm, Vol 14, No 3)
Broadheads vs. Field Points by Robin Klemme (AFm, Vol 4, No 3)

The Diamong Infinite Edge, adjustable from 13″ to 30″ of draw and 5# to 70# of draw weight!

Still More on Coaching Archery

Chapter 18
Ultra-Adjustable Compound Bows

Looking for "The" Step-Up" Bow

I have written before of the need for a quality, low-cost bow for archers to "step up" into after their initial archery experience ("We Need an Adult Beginner's Compound" in AFm 13-4 and in **More on Coaching Archery**, Watching Arrows Fly, 2010). That initial experience is today often with a zero-letoff compound bow like the Mathews *Genesis*, so this first "real" compound bow is quite a different breed.

Enter into the market what I am calling "ultra-adjustable bows." Gone are the days where compounds came with 3″ of draw length adjustment and 15-25% of peak weight reduction. The first example of this kind of bow that was brought to my attention was the Diamond *Infinite Edge*, which featured draw length settings adjustable between 13 and 30 inches without changing the limbs or using a bow press! Wow! On top of that was a draw weight range between 5 and 70 pounds! Holy smokes! Quick on the heels of whoever was first into this new market were similar bows from many of the bow manufacturers (*see the sidebar "Some Ultra-Adjustables Now Available" below*).

Was this the answer to my plea?

There is Some Cloud Along with that Silver Lining

The specs for the *Infinite Edge* were quite impressive: "with a 31-inch axle-to-axle length and a seven-inch brace height, the 3.1-pound Infinite Edge can shoot arrows at speeds up to 310 feet per second," but . . . the short ATA means that this bow really needs to be shot with a release aid. The reason? Finger pinch. The *Genesis* compound has a roughly 36″ ATA but what makes it "finger friendly" is its low draw weight. With a maximum of 20# (25# on the *Genesis Pro*) there isn't that much tension on the bow string, so you don't get that much finger pinch. But when the draw weight goes up, the string tension goes up with it, and if the ATA gets smaller the string angles get tighter and . . . ouch. If you look through the specs for the bows in the sidebar, you will see that the ATA lengths of all but one are between 27″ and 31″; in a word "really short."

So, BFD, they just need to buy a release, no? No. They need to buy a release and learn to use it. And maybe they should have a peep sight and, well, a bow sight, and might as well include a stabilizer as they are allowed, and now the purchase of a "next" bow has doubled in cost and more than doubled in training time. It is all well and good that you can start your own child with a full compound rig as you will be there to supervise their every shot, but for those not having a full time supervisor/coach, we still recommend that beginners start shooting "barebow/fingers" and add accessories one at a time, so they can evaluate whether they like them . . . and whether they can afford them.

A big drawback of these bows was that all of the draw weights were not available at all of the draw lengths. In general, the longer the draw, the higher the draw weight, and sometimes the "minimum" at an archer's draw length was over the "maximum" that beginning archer could pull. This is a big problem . . .

. . . which might have been solved by the new Parker *Lightning*.

While Parker claims for its new ultra-adjustable bow that "all draw weights are available at all draw lengths" I haven't yet seen that with my own eyes. I am trying to get a review of that bow for *Archery Focus*, so stay tuned.

What Parker also did brilliantly is hit the price point perfectly. They priced the *Lightning* at $299.95. With the market-leading "beginner" compound, the Genesis, selling anywhere from $135-$200, this is the perfect "step up" from that price point without having to jump to the $400-$500 bows typical of the market.

Still it would be nice to have some target colors, Parker. (I believe in asking for what you want.)

What's At Stake

Archery is going through one of its many resurgences. Archery is more popular than it has been in recent memory. Since only a small number out of every 100 who try archery (at school and various fun shoots and other venues) actually stick with our sport, an archer kept is worth many dozens of just prospective archers. Think about how many more compound archers we might keep if, after their initial compound experience, they were able to purchase a fairly high-performance bow that can be adjusted with simple hand tools to fit them properly and then can be refit to them, again with simple hand tools, when they grow in height (and therefore draw length) or strength through better technique. And if $400 would get them such a bow and a dozen arrows and a good tab?

The Archery Trade Association (ATA) has done studies that show how much the "average" archer spends on equipment and such throughout their participation in archery. Keeping people in the sport once hooked is certainly a way to maximize revenues and keep the sport growing. So, it should be worth it to offer such bows at these low price points. (Also brand loyalty is being built.) Keeping it simple is a tried and true path.

And just to be complete, here (again) are the specs I think are perfect for a step-up compound bow:

A Step-Up Compound Bow is . . .

A Step-Up Compound is Affordable Ideally it would have a MSRP of $299 or less, but anything under $350 would be nice.

A Step-Up Compound has a Low Draw Weight Ideally it would have a peak weight of 40 pounds that could be cranked down to 30. Making the jump from a learner's bow of 20 pounds of draw to 50 pounds of draw just isn't fun. Motivated bowhunters, young and old, are eager to get to 40-50 pounds of draw as that is often considered a minimum draw weight at which to hunt bigger game, but recreational archers are in it for the fun and a high draw weight isn't desirable and certainly isn't necessary.

A Step-Up Compound has a Minimum of 39-40 Inches Axle-to-Axle Almost all beginners learn to shoot on a low draw weight bow with their fingers on the string. Most enjoy the feeling of being in control of the bowstring. Also, ask any of the release shooters you know, "Did you shoot a release from the beginning?" and you'll hear a great many say "No, I shot "fingers" before." Modern compound bows are designed for release-shooting hunters who hunt in dense brush or from tree stands and are therefore too short for "fingers" shooters.

A Step-Up Compound has a Letoff of 50%-60% Yes I said fifty (5-0) percent. These bows are designed for archers who learned to shoot on 15-20 pound recurve bows (typically). With a 28-inch draw, one has 20 pounds "in hand" when shooting a twenty pound recurve bow. A 35-pound compound bow with 50% letoff gives an archer 17 pounds "in hand," which is plenty to get a clean release off of the string. Obviously anything in the 50%-60% range will work well, but 70%–80% letoff on a low-drawing bow does not provide enough tension on the string at full draw to get a clean release of the string.

A Step-Up Compound has a Draw Length Easily Reset to a Wide Range of Draws It would be well that the draw length adjustments require nothing more complicated than an Allen wrench—no bow press, no cable twisting, etc. – either a single moveable module (ideal) or a set of draw length modules that come with the bow (acceptable). I think a range from 26-31 inches should cover the vast majority of adult beginners. The youth and short-draw adult market will cover the lower end and those of us with Gorilla Arms (of whom I am one) will just have to spend more money (as do people who wear over-sized clothes, over-sized shoes, etc.).

Some Ultra-Adjustables Now Available

Parker
2014 *Lightning*
Brace Height: 7″
Draw Length Range: 19″ – 29″ (in 1/2″ increments)
Draw Weight: 30-60 lbs.
Speed: 310 fps
Axle to Axle: 30″
Effective Let-Off: 70%
Weight: 3.45 lbs.

Diamond
2013 *Infinite Edge*
Brace Height: 7″
Draw Length Range: 13″ – 30″
Draw Weight: 5–70 lbs.
Speed: 308 fps
Kinetic Energy: 74.7 ft. per lbs.
Axle to Axle: 31″
Effective Let-Off: 75%
Weight: 3.1 lbs.

Bear
2013 *Apprentice 2*
Speed (IBO): 265 Fps

Weight: 2.9 Lbs
Brace Height: 6.125″
Axle To Axle: 27.5″
Peak Draw Weight: 15 - 60 lbs
Draw Length Range: 15″ to 27″
Let-Off: 70%

2013 *Outbreak*
Speed (IBO): 308 Fps
Weight: 3.5 Lbs
Brace Height: 7.25″
Axle To Axle: 29.25″
Peak Draw Weight: 15 - 70 lbs
Draw Length Range: 16″ to 30″
Let-Off: 80%

Mission
2013 *Menace*
Weight: 2.95 lbs.
Axle to Axle: 31″
Brace Height: 7.25″
Let-off: Up to 70%
Draw Weight: 16 - 52 lbs.
Draw Length: 17" - 30″
MSRP: $269

2013 *Craze*
IBO Rate: Up to 306 fps
Weight: 3.6 lbs.
Axle to Axle: 28″
Brace Height: 7.5″
Let-off: 80%
Draw Weight: 15 - 70 lbs
Draw Length: 19" - 30″
MSRP: $299

2013 *Riot*
IBO Rate: Up to 310 fps
Weight: 4.3 lbs.
Axle to Axle: 31″
Brace Height: 7″
Let-off: Up to 80%
Draw Weight: 15 - 70 lbs
Draw Length: 19" - 30″
MSRP: $399

2013 *Rally*
IBO Rate: Up to 300 FPS
Weight: 4 lbs.
Axle to Axle: 37″
Brace Height: 7.25″
Let-off: Up to 75%
Draw Weight: 26-70 lbs
Draw Length: 22″-30″
MSRP: $499

Hoyt
2013 *Ruckus*
Axle-To-Axle: 29½″
Brace Height: 6½″
Draw Weight: 10-40#, 20-50#
Weight: 2.8 Lbs.
Draw Lengths: 18″-28″

All specs were taken from the manufacturers' websites in early 2014 and are subject to change.

Additional Learning References
How Compound Bows Mislead Beginners by Steve Ruis (AFm, Vol 17, No 3)
We Need an Adult Beginner's Compound by Steve Ruis (AFm, Vol 13, No 4)
The Ignition—*Mathews Step-up Youth Compound* by Ava McDowell (AFm, Vol 10, No 5)

EASTON OUTDOOR & INDOOR TARGET • FIELD • 3-D ARROW SELECTION CHART

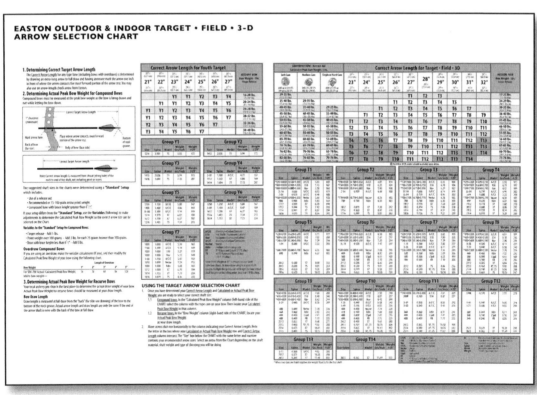

Every coach needs to learn his or her way around an arrow spine chart. This is Eastons Target Archery Spine Chart from 2004. (Hey, it was the one I had handy; it isn't as if you are going to use it!)

Chapter 19
What the Coach Training Classes Leave Out . . . and Shouldn't

I have been critical of our coach training programs in the past primarily because they don't teach you how to coach. For example, coaching positions are described, along with what you can and can't see from each . . . and then the topic is dropped. They don't say how to evaluate a new archer, where to begin, what is most important to check first, etc. These classes are focused on teaching coaches how arrows are properly shot and not on how to teach archers to shoot arrows properly.

In talking with a recent coach trainee, I realized there is another large area in these programs that could be improved. And any youth archery coach can tell you what it is. After you have taught a youth how to shoot with basic, solid T-Form, what is the next subject they want to talk about? Do you know?

It's how to go about getting their own archery gear (bow, arrows, etc.). Given that most coaches are either archery parents, or older archers wanting to give something back to the sport, how prepared are they to give advice to beginners about equipment? Answer: not very.

Let's look at this.

Gearing Up
In our training programs we use the event of a beginning archer (of any age) getting their own equipment as the borderline between being a "Beginner" and being an "Intermediate" Archer. This does not mean someone can walk off of the street into an archery shop, buy a bow and some arrows, and be deemed an intermediate archer on the spot. This is because if you don't have some semblance of basically good form, no one can fit you properly for archery gear. Our intrepid wannabe intermediate archer is really just a shopper.

The value of having one's own gear over borrowed program equipment (which was chosen primarily for reasons of safety, durability, flexibility, and cost) is that one's own gear can be "fitted" to provide superior performance. The fitting, though, has to take into account the abilities of the specific archer: a bow too big, too heavy, or with too much draw weight will ruin an archer's developing form. If they end up spending a lot of money on equipment that they cannot handle, that creates resentment, not satisfaction.

So, what's a coach to do?

Giving Equipment Advice

Here is a common scenario, one I am working through right now with several of my private students. They need additional gear or replacement gear and their parents control the purse strings. The student doesn't know what they need (though they may know what they want) and the parent is often bewildered about the whole thing. And you, the coach, don't know what the family's resources are, what their budget for recreation is, etc.

Some Teachable Principles for Equipment Recommendations

Some aspects of this issue are quite general and are addressed here. More specific recommendations follow below.

• *If at All Possible, "Try Before You Buy"*
Any parent knows that their kids "just have to have" this thingamajig or other. And when they finally get their heart's desire, it isn't quite what they expected or their interest shifts onto something else. Sporting goods are notorious for living out most of their life spans on garage shelves. (If you have kids go out right now into your garage and look at what you have stored there and I will bet there are more than a few pieces of sporting equipment bought and then interest was lost.) The companion to this principle is . . .

• *Let Youths Earn New Equipment*
Parents often try to encourage their kids to pursue endeavors they approve of by buying them the wherewithal to participate. I think this sends the wrong message. Instead, let them "earn" new gear through their participation, in classes or independent practice. This is a much better sign that the equipment is really needed (as opposed to just wanted—who doesn't like new gear, really?).

• *Youths Need to Be Fit with their Growth in Mind*
Youths who have not reached their full size need to be fitted with their growth in mind. As one simple example, when buying a compound bow for a youth, both the draw weight and draw length need to be able to be adjusted upward. Why? Because as a youth gets taller, her draw length goes up accordingly (about one half inch per inch of height) and as she ages, she gets stronger and the draw weight she can handle goes up. So, compound bows should be picked so that the lowest draw weight and draw length settings are near what the archer can do now. If they are instead near the tops of those ranges, a new bow is going to be needed shortly.

The same is true for arrows. I tend to size arrows about two spine groups too stiff and then cut them two inches too long to compensate. This allows for the archer's draw length to go up and if a stiffer arrow is needed they can be cut somewhat to stiffen them up.

• *All Coaches Need to Educate Themselves about Equipment*
Most of us specialize as archers and as coaches. I came up in archery as a compound archer. Because of demand for coaching services, I learned recurve and longbow archery. In addition I had to educate myself (an ongoing effort) about what beginner and intermediate level equipment is available/desirable in all of those disciplines.

In order to learn about those styles, I acquired longbows (I have four now) and recurve bows (a half a dozen, the best being a Hoyt *GMX* with a 27″ riser) because archery is a kinesthetic sport. It is all about feel, so if you want to teach a style, you have to shoot it yourself. Many of these are used as training bows. I have right-handed and left-handed polymer-riser bows with 10#, 14-16#, and 22# limbs that I use when working with all kinds of archers. (My current favorite is the Cartel model.) I start rank

Still More on Coaching Archery

beginners with a 10# bow until they have learned good body positioning, then we swap in 14# limbs, etc.

I have a student who wants to take a shot at making an Olympic team; I shocked him by handing him the 10# bow and asked him to shoot it. By doing that I was able to convince him that he had an overly muscular shot (you really have to relax to shoot a 10# bow successfully), which helped me convince him to drop 12# of draw weight while we rebuilt his shot.

Where did I learn to do this? Unfortunately, not in coach training programs.

A Beginning on Establishing Specific Equipment Recommendations

In the conversation mentioned above, the brand new Level 3-NTS coach had told me that previously, as a recurve archer, anything said about compound bows just kind of went in one ear and out the other. She assumed the compound specialist would handle those needs. Well— surprise!—there are no compound specialists in her JOAD program. She paid more attention in her latest training and is starting to pick some things up. But, I argue, what she needs to know isn't covered in her courses (or made available on web sites or newsletters). Here are some specific equipment recommendations with background information (needed by people not in the know).

- *Recurve Bows Need to Be Fitted for Bow Length and Draw Weight*
  Growing archers probably need a little more length than normal. If you stand a strung bow on your shoe top, it is the right length for target archery if the other tip is between nose and chin. An inch or two more of growth room is fine. That length is about 3-4 inches shorter than the "length" of the bow on its label as recurve bows are measured when strung along the curved back of the bow (from string notch to string notch). If you are going to make a mistake in guessing what draw weight limbs to get, erring on the low side is best. Have your student try higher draw weight bows and see where they start "trying" (not struggling, but when they start exerting themselves so they look like they aren't struggling). Back off a couple of pounds from there.

- *There is Nothing Wrong with Wooden-risered Recurve Bows*
  All of the really cool recurve bows have metal risers. But for beginners and intermediate archers, especially youths, there is absolutely nothing wrong with recurve bows with wood risers. (Traditional recurve archers pay many hundreds of dollars for bows with wood risers; if they also didn't shoot well I don't think you would see that happening.)

  In fact, wood recurves have several advantages over metal-risered recurve bows. For one they are lighter. This is especially important because after the string is loosed during a shot the entire weight of the bow and everything attached to it (sights, stabilizers, etc.) has to be held up by the bow arm and the muscles for this are not particularly well developed in youths.

  For another, such bows are much less expensive, which means the archer's archery budget can be used to buy other accessories (sights, stabilizers, etc.), which can, of course, be attached to a metal-risered bow after some future upgrade.

  Some of the wood bows are quite beautiful (but not shiny and sparkly like the metal ones).

- *Three-piece Recurve Bows are the Most Practical Recurves*
  They are because when a limb change is needed you can just buy new limbs instead of a whole new bow. Such "take down" bows are easier to pack for trips, too.

- *When Fitting Compound Bows, Fit to the Minimums* (Beginners and Growing Youths)

As mentioned above, the growing archer's maximum draw weight and current draw length should be near the *minimum* settings available on the bow. Compound bows have their own draw weight and length ranges, which must be adjusted to precisely match those of the archer.

- *Lighter Arrows Fly Faster and Farther*

Youths and short-draw adults often struggle in target archery when the distances get long. This problem is referred to as "making distance." The problem comes from low arrow speeds, which result from low draw weights and short draw lengths (the energy entering the arrow is based upon the force applied to the arrow (partially related to draw weight) and the distance the arrow travels under that force (partially related to draw length)). If the arrow doesn't receive much "oomph" from the bow then the archer has to aim higher to get the arrow to the target. If the angle is too great, the point of aim is off the target and there is a loss of accuracy; and tilting the body at a large angle loses quality of execution, which hurts consistency. The least expensive equipment fix for this problem is the purchase of lighter arrows.

Many beginners start with arrows that were designed for durability and safety. For example the Genesis arrow is an 1820 aluminum arrow (the 18 refers to the diameter of the arrow in 64^{ths} of an inch and the 20 refers to the thickness of the aluminum shafts wall in thousandths of an inch). This arrow is generally shot full length, so the arrow protrudes out quite far in front of the bow. This wall thickness ($20/1000$ of an inch) is typical of heavy-duty hunting arrows. "Target arrows" have wall thicknesses of 14, 13, or even 12 (thousandths of an inch). For early learners, a 14 wall is a good choice as a blend of durability and lighter weight. The diameter then determines what is called the shaft's "spine" which is a measure of the shaft's resilience or "stiffness." As a general rule, the greater the draw weight, the stiffer the arrow needs to be. To make things as confusing as possible, the *lower* the spine number, the *stiffer* the arrow shaft is and vice-versa.

Lighter than "target weight" aluminum shafts are "all carbon" shafts. (There are shafts made of both aluminum and carbon, so there is lots to learn here.) In general, carbon shafts are lighter, stiffer, and more expensive than comparably-sized aluminum shafts. Aluminum shafts can be bent, but then can be straightened (a time or two); carbon shafts generally can't be bent, but when they are damaged they cannot be fixed as easily as aluminum shafts or at all.

In general compound bows can shoot arrows with a wider range of spines than recurve bows, but if there is a mismatch in spine, forget about being able to fit that arrow to that bow and archer in a way that maximizes the success as an archer. A "spine match" is absolutely essential to a well-fitted arrow.

- *You Need to Learn Your Way Around an Arrow Spine Chart*

I don't care which spine chart you study. (I recommend Easton's as they make more arrows than anybody else, see first page of this chapter.) What you will find in any of these charts is this. The columns list different draw lengths in inches. The rows list different draw weights, generally in five-pound increments. Then the boxes at the intersection of each draw length (plus or minus one half inch) and draw weight (plus or minus two and a half pounds of draw weight) contain either the manufacturer's arrow models or, in Easton's case (because they make so many different kinds of arrows), they list a "spine group" which is just a label for a list of their various arrows that have the proper spine at that length.

Still More on Coaching Archery

The key thing about these charts (all of them) is that the arrow spines or spine groups will be found listed on a 45-degree angle through the chart. This is basically because they have designed the arrows so that "five pounds of draw roughly equates to one inch of draw." As an example of this equivalence, if you decide you want to crank your compound bow up five more pounds of draw weight, and you have well over one inch of arrow sticking out past your arrow rest at full draw, you can simply cut one inch off of those arrows and they will shoot just as well as the last setup did. If you go up 2.5 pounds, cut off one half of an inch, etc. (Obviously if you lower the draw weight, there is no way to lengthen the arrow to compensate for that effect, so other less effective measures need to be tried.) But once a shaft has been selected, there is nothing that compares to shaft length in adjusting the arrow's spine.

- *Too Much Draw Weight Kills Good Form*
I can't say this strongly enough. Too much draw weight too soon distorts archery form and diminishes the desire to participate. People have been saying this for centuries.

- *You Need a Serving Tool*
Coaches need to acquire a serving tool and some spools of serving thread. Bowstrings wear out the center serving about three times faster than the rest of the string, so removing and replacing a center serving is a common thing. And once you master that task, there is little more you need to know to make your own strings and cables.

- *Shooting Compound Bows with Mechanical Releases Is Very Different from with Fingers*
For one the draw length setting can be ½" to 1" different. The arrows needed can be quite different. And "release" shooters have a wider range of acceptable arrow spines than do "fingers" shooters.

- *There is Nothing Wrong with Wooden-risered Recurve Bows (Part 2)*
I see a great many young archers rush from lighter wood- and polymer-risered recurve bows into metal-risered bows because that's what "other people" have. But often these growing archers do not have enough upper arm development to hold those heavier bows up through the shot, so they get months of practice "dropping their bow arms", which we do not want. If you ask any top archer whether they would prefer a cheap riser with good limbs attached or a good riser with cheap limbs attached, 99 out of 100 would say the "cheap riser with good limbs" (the other one is just a weirdo). The limbs are far more important than the riser. Make sure your young archers have a good reason and the musculature for moving to a heavier bow.

- *Carbon is Not Like Bacon: It Does Not Make Everything Better*
Archers act like the opposite is true. They are always ready to buy something if carbon (in the form of carbon fibers) is somehow incorporated. While carbon does make everything more expensive, there may be no benefit to a learning archer and there may even be negatives. The best carbon purchase is when shooting for distance and needing lighter arrows to maintain good form. The other uses can wait.

Working with Local Shops
If you are blessed to have a high quality-archery shop nearby, take advantage. Go by the shop and check it out. Talk to the staff; introduce yourself. Ask if there is a specialist on staff who works with beginners a lot, so you can refer your students to that person. Ask your students for feedback on their equipment experiences and pass that along to the shop (with kudos if the service is good). Shop owners don't always get direct feedback except from unhappy customers, so be sure to pass along the good stuff when you hear it.

Additional Learning References

A Parent's Guide to Archery by Steve Ruis (WAF, 2012) This book provides parents an orientation to the sport and our equipment.

Archery Coaching How To's by Steve Ruis (WAF 2014) This book provides teaching protocols for coaches teaching outside of the primary fields (compound for recurve coaches, etc.).

Setting Up New Archery Gear by AER (AFm, Vol 14, No 6)

Buying New Archery Gear by AER (AFm, Vol 14, No 5)

Simple Maintenance for Archery—A Book Review by Steve Ruis (AFm, Vol 17, No 3) All coaches need a copy of this book (reviewed here), now out in a second edition (New! Improved!) and no, I didn't write it (wish I had).

Cool Archery Gear You Can Get 'At the Store' by Steve Ruis (AFm, Vol 8, No 1)

Finding the Right Equipment by Rick McKinney (AFm, Vol 5, No 4)

To test the idea of "up crawls" I added a few extra nocking point locators to create additional nocking points . . . above the normal positions for such.

Still More on Coaching Archery

Chapter 20
A Stringwalking Puzzle

At a recent Illinois Target Archery Association Indoor Championships, a friend came up with a question that created more questions than it answered. I had told him that a Recurve Barebow setup is best tuned starting at the "point on" target distance and then adjusted to get reasonable arrow flight with the longest crawl. My friend replied that he had a colleague who had "tuned his setup to be optimal at 18 m" for the indoor season.

My mind just spun trying to imagine how one would do that: tuned for best arrow flight? smallest groups? by bare shaft? So, I decided to go back to square one regarding the dynamics of the situation and this is what came to me.

Geometry Issues

Consider the recurve bow at brace in the figure. The horizontal centerline of the bow is usually in line with the pivot point of the grip. This creates the situation that the arrow rest position is above the center of the bow about as much as the center of pressure (COP) of the bow hand is below it. (Ideally these two would be at the same position but this is impossible unless you have a hole in your hand big enough for the arrow to pass through.) The nocking point is about one-half inch above the level of the arrow rest, so that the arrow (depending on size) is centered about ⅜″ above level and an additional inch and a half or so above the previously mentioned centerline. All of these are examples of the various tradeoffs necessary to design a bow (*see illustration*).

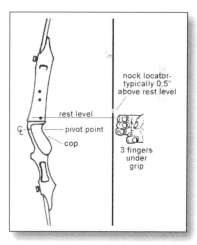

Basically this means the archer's fingers (plus tab), being 2″-2.5″ wide, are close to being centered on the bowstring or slightly above center (*see fingers in diagram in relation to bow's centerline (CL)*). Of course, the bow hand is on the bottom half of the bow, creating the familiar tiller problem: by holding the bow asymmetrically, that is with the bow hand on the bottom half and the string hand near center (or higher if split finger grip used), we in effect have made the top limb longer (and therefore weaker than the bottom limb). Many people adjust for this by adjusting the tiller of the bow by turning the top limb bolt to create a slightly stronger limb on top than bottom. (The word tiller means the same in archery as in boating; it means a thing "to steer.") Others address this issue by adjusting the nocking point location, leaving the limb bolts alone. If you move the nocking point up, you are decreasing the leverage you have on the top limb, making it effectively stronger, and apparently only small adjustments in nocking point location are necessary to adjust for the problem that comes from holding the bow on its bottom half.

For outdoors, I had recommended tuning at "point-on-target distance" (*archaic* "point blank range") and then adjusting to get reasonable arrow flight at the largest crawls. But what about indoors, where there is one and only one crawl as most people shoot the whole season at one and only one distance: 18 m/20 yd?

Some address this situation by trying to create a setup that has 18 m as its "point on," that is, the point-on-target distance when using the arrow point to aim with. To get the smallest crawl, arrows are shot full length in that the farther the arrow sticks out in front of the bow, the lower the bow must be held to get it on target (because the arrow slopes upward from below the aiming eye forward; the farther upward it sticks, the lower the bow must be held to get the point onto the target). Also, heavier arrows are used because the heavier the arrow, the slower it goes and lower it hits on the target. This is accomplished by adding weight tubes into shafts or loading up the points with lead, or both. Typically, since arrows are selected to be shot full length and with very heavy points, they need to be also quite stiff/heavy. If this is pulled off, you have a shot with no or very little crawl.

But what if this doesn't appeal or the weight of the arrow is so excessive that it seems untunable? What came to me is that the traditional approach (tune at "point on," adjust for acceptable arrow flight at largest crawl), which works fine for outdoors, is less than fine for indoors. You take a bow with bowhand on the bottom half (which requires tiller and/or nocking point locator adjustments to deal with) and by taking a crawl, you are moving your string hand onto the bottom half of the string, which exacerbates everything. So, the thought occurred: why not leave your string hand where it was and just move the arrow up?

To test this, I created a bowstring with multiple nocking point locators. (Only two are allowed in competition, but "This is a test, this is only a test! Were this a real emergency. . .") This created a series of "up crawls"(?) spaced about ⅜" apart. I wanted to test small, medium, and large "up crawls," so this seemed appropriate.

The bottom nocking point locator is the bottom locator already on the string and tells me where my fingers would be at my "point on" distance before. I then simply added additional nocking point locators spaced so that I could get an arrow nock in between them (*see photo opposite first page of this chapter*).

The plan was to shoot arrows at the indoor distance and evaluate (a) whether clean shots can be made and (b) where they land on the target. If the bow was reasonably tuned to start with, I should be able to get reasonable arrow flight somewhere near where my arrow was positioned relative to my fingers from before (my old crawl) but with the arrow simply moved up and the fingers left where they were. If this works, I expect the result would be improved with tiller adjustments, which would then be a follow-up experiment.

To evaluate the tests I decided to check two things: the sound of the bow and the hit points of the arrows. Later I might be able to include high-speed video of the strings during the shot.

The results . . . to be published in *Archery Focus* magazine!)

Additional Learning References

How to Teach Stringwalking by AER (AFm, Vol 18, No 1)
Sighting In for Barebow by John R. Templar (AFm, Vol 11, No 6)
Tuning a Compound Bow for Stringwalking by John R. Templar (AFm, Vol 11, No 5)

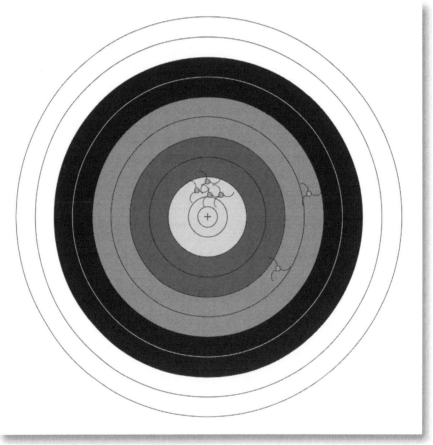

Can you tell what caused this group of six arrows? Is it even a group?

Still More on Coaching Archery

Chapter 21
Can You Read Arrow Patterns?

Archers and especially coaches can benefit greatly from being able to read the patterns arrows make in a target. In this chapter I will go through master lists of things that can cause groups to be off center: each category will then be broken into causes that are rooted in the archer's equipment and causes that are rooted in the archer's form and execution. Occasionally I will mention issues that are rooted in the archer's mental game. Before I do that, however, there are some cautions.

The Law of Small Numbers You must be aware that sets of small numbers or events often show substantial differences. For example, if you flipped a penny six times, what do you think the outcome would be? Most people say three heads and three tails. If you tried this and got six straight tails, would you begin to question that coin? If you would, then you are one of the people Las Vegas was set up to get rich off of. Getting six straight heads or tails is not that rare an occurrence. Flip a set of six enough and you will get one such set fairly often. I say fairly often because you think that should be a rare occurrence when it really is not.

So if an archer shoots a smallish group to the left of center, does that indicate anything? Maybe yes, maybe no. Three straight groups like that and I would be looking for a cause. For some archers, just one such arrow would have me looking for a cause. These latter archers are those who shoot small groups, dead center almost all of the time. But for an intermediate archer or even some advanced archers, make sure you have seen enough shots to show they are consistently high or low or left or right of where they want to be.

Rarely is There Just One Thing Wrong Unless you are dealing with a very advanced archer, it is rare that there is just one thing wrong. I usually approach this by trying to fix one part of an archer's shot and then see the outcome. If they were consistently high and left and you made a change and now they are consistently just left, you did fix part of the problem but you need to fix the other part of the problem; there is more work to do.

Coaches Need to Know Why Tuning recurve bows is all about when and where the arrow leaves the string. If the arrow leaves the string too soon or too late, you will have a bad tune and left or right groups. This point is determined by a match between the dynamic arrow spine, the arrow mass, and the brace height of the bow. If you raise the brace height, the arrow comes off sooner. If you lower it, it comes off later. (You can watch this with a high-speed camera.)

Knowing why a certain change affects an arrow will be critical in being able to diagnose a "cure" for what ails your archer or your archer's setup and tune.

Caveats All of the descriptions below are for right-handed archers. If you are a lefty, you have to reverse all right-left axes. (Sorry, lefties.) Also, we assume that a basically good setup as a starting point here: the bow is set up well, and the arrows are all the same weight, the same length, all arrow components in line, etc. There is no sense in diagnosing target patterns if there are known issues in the bow and arrows. Fix them first.

Group shooting at distance is diagnostic because at longer distances things show up that do not at shorter ones for the simple fact that the longer an arrow flies off line, the farther it gets from target center.

High Groups

Equipment Sources

- nocking point too low
- arrow riding up sloping arrow rest
- stiffer lower limb on bow
- arrow moving down string during draw or release
- loose aperture (dropping down)
- loose sight mounting block (dropping down)

Form and Execution Sources

- bow hand too low on grip or "heeling the bow"
- bow hand/arm jerking up on release
- bow arm extended more than usual (recurves and longbows)
- overdrawing bow (recurves and longbows)
- fingers pinching down on arrow nock (finger release)
- string hand drawing down at release (finger release)
- greater pressure taken on the third finger (finger release)
- flicking fingers down on release (finger release)
- rolling release–top to bottom (finger release)
- draw elbow elevation too high
- having an open mouth, lowering chin position (finger release)

Mental Sources

- freezing, a form of target panic in which the archer cannot move their aperture onto target center and are "frozen" in one spot, here above the target center. The archer should be able to describe this but some are too embarrassed to admit this.

Low Groups

Equipment Sources

- arrow nocking point too high
- arrow dropping off rest on release
- stiffer upper limb on bow
- armguard or clothing catching on bowstring
- nocks out of round on shaft
- clearance problem: fletches hitting bow or rest on release
- arrow moving up string during draw or release
- weight variations in arrows
- FOC variation in arrows
- string stretching

Form and Execution Sources

- grip higher on bow, e.g. high wrist grip instead of other
- dropping bow arm on release
- bow arm bent more than usual (recurve and longbow)
- bow shoulder raised (recurve and longbow)
- draw hand rolling, flinching or double release (finger release)
- dead or static release, when live release is usual (finger release)
- forward release (finger release)
- rolling release–bottom to top (finger release)
- more pressure on index finger than usual (finger release)
- fingers pinching arrow nock (finger release)
- plucking fingers off string (also left error)
- shooting through clicker (finger release)

Mental Sources

- freezing, a form of target panic in which the archer cannot move their aperture onto target center and are "frozen" in one spot, here below the target center. The archer should be able to describe this but some are too embarrassed to admit this.

(con't next page)

Right Groups

Equipment Sources

- nocks too loose or too tight on string
- nocks out of round on shaft
- arrow shaft too weak
- worn arrow rest
- clearance problem: fletches hitting bow or rest on release
- bow brace height too low
- bow limbs twisted (recurve and longbow)
- bow limbs not aligned (recurve and longbow)
- bow limbs very loose (recurve and longbow)
- arrow rest in too far
- button pressure too weak
- arrow rest too far forward or back (not L or R)

Form and Execution Sources

- torquing bow to the right
- canting top limb to the right
- string alignment too far left
- shooting through clicker
- twisting torso to the right upon release

Mental Sources

- freezing, a form of target panic in which the archer cannot move their aperture onto target center and are "frozen" in one spot, here to the right of target center. The archer should be able to describe this but some are too embarrassed to admit this.

Left Groups

Equipment Sources

- nocks too loose or too tight on string
- nocks out of round on shaft

Still More on Coaching Archery

- arrow shaft too stiff
- worn arrow rest
- clearance problem: fletches hitting bow or rest on release
- bow limbs twisted (recurve and longbow)
- bow limbs not aligned (recurve and longbow)
- arrow rest out too far
- button pressure too stiff
- arrow rest too far forward or back (not L or R)

Form and Execution Sources

- plucking the release
- torquing bow to the left
- canting top limb to the left
- string alignment too far right
- shooting through clicker
- twisting torso to the left upon release
- leaning backwards
- bowstring hitting arm guard/clothing on release
- loss of back tension on release

Mental Sources

- freezing, a form of target panic in which the archer cannot move their aperture onto target center and are "frozen" in one spot, here to the right of target center. The archer should be able to describe this but some are too embarrassed to admit this.

Particularly helpful in compiling these lists was the Centenary Archers Club web site (from www.centenaryarchers.gil.com.au/coaching.htm) in Australia, which I recommend to you.

Additional Learning References

How to Adjust Tiller for Maximum Recurve Bow Performance by Don Rabska (AFm, Vol 18, No 1)
Indoor Spots and Indoor Bows by Larry Wise (AFm, Vol 15, No 6)
A "Simple Tech" Approach to Group Tuning by Steve Ruis (AFm, Vol 14, No 4)
The Problem with Walk Back Tuning by Joe Tapley (AFm, Vol 13, No 1)
Tuning by Tyler Benner (AFm, Vol 8, No 5)
The French Method of Tuning by Steve Ruis (AFm, Vol 8, No 4)

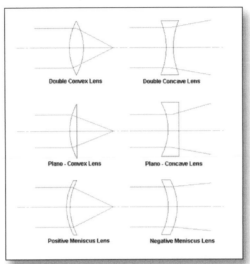

Various lens shapes do things to images. For "scopes" the two most common are the top two in the left column.

The circular "pin guard" original sold as a way to protect one's pin from getting bent, was always designed to help the archer line up the hole in the peep with the sight itself resulting in more precise aiming.

Still More on Coaching Archery

Chapter 22
The Optics of Apertures

There is a sizeable quantity of BS (I don't know what else to call it . . . misinformation?. . . seems too prissy) in almost every aspect of archery. It seems as if there is more than the usual amount when it comes to sight apertures.

The recurve people have fewer choices because they are not allowed any magnification; basically they are allowed a sight pin or a sight ring to aim with. Most people agree that the ring is superior because of our hard-wired mental subroutine that allows us to recognize lines that are parallel and circles that are concentric (necessary for distance estimation and determining angle of view). For example, if you look down a tunnel or pipe, if the far end's edge (a circle) is concentric to the near end's edge (another circle), then you are looking straight down the pipe. If the far circle is to the right, you are looking down the left, etc. Aperture rings are round, as are most target rings, so your brain automatically self-centers the circle of the aperture on the circles of the target rings (making them concentric). Since your attention is on target center, the aperture ring (typically outside of the cone of focus of your eyes) shows less apparent movement and therefore seems steadier. Lines itself up with the target, seems steadier, . . . is there any dispute?

The only remaining question is should you look at the aperture (and have the target out of focus) or look at the target (and have the aperture out of focus). There are many hardened opinions out there for you to read if you want, but there are also many archers who have been very successful using either approach, so my recommendation is: try them both to see if you have a preference. Put on a practice tournament and see if you get better scores looking at the target or looking at your aperture. If you prove to yourself that one does better than the other, I can't see how that can do anything but help you.

For compound people . . . aye, there's the rub!

The Optics of Compound Bow Sights
Compound bow sights are generally a pin, or multiple pins, or a "scope" which is a abbreviation of "telescopic aperture." Additional advantages are provided by peep sites that come with and without magnification.

The Pin Sight Most pin sights have multiple pins, which is an advantage to bow hunters. Having a single pin or scope requires the aperture to be moved for various distances shot, which is why such sights are often referred to as "moveable sights" versus "fixed pin sights." Having a set of pins, each one sighted in for a different distance, makes for a versatile sight that can cover a wide range of distances but doesn't require any fiddling as a deer walks into range.

Most of these sights have acquired a circular "pin housing" over the years that allows more effective use of a peep sight (*see below*). First, like most equipment innovations in archery, such pin housings were a form of cheating. Now they are standard equipment (*see photo*).

Other than that, the issues are the same as for recurve archers shooting with pins/small loops.

Well, there is one difference. Some pin sights use fiber optic "pins" that gather a great deal of light and pump it down the fiber to emerge as a glowing dot at the end of fiber. In bright sunlight, these glowing dots appear much larger than in very dim light and can throw off archers by creating a different sight picture. While they can be a positive benefit in low-light conditions where one's pins might be very hard to see, this "nuclear glow" in direct sunlight causes some to avoid them. (I stopped using them for this reason, so I might be a little prejudiced on this topic.)

Telescopic Apertures I don't know when it was that "scopes" became popular or even accepted. I assume it was quite recently (the 1970s?). In compound archery, shooting with a scope is now the most common style by far. So, why aren't archers more knowledgeable about scopes and how they work? (Psst, I think it is because there is some math involved.)

The Optics of Scopes

So what does a scope do and how does it do it? Scopes are fairly simple optically. They are little magnifying glasses (with long focal lengths). If you have a magnifying glass, get it out; it will make things easier to understand. If you look at something through the magnifying glass (typically this is a double convex lens meaning it is thicker in the middle than the edges), as you move the magnifying lens a little farther away from you it will reach a point where the image flips over to be upside down. Archery scopes are like this but they have very long focal lengths, meaning the point at which the image flips over is very far from the lens. You could imagine it being quite disconcerting to find at a long shot the image was upside down! So, this is not desired and it was designed out.

Most archery scopes are either this double-convex design or plano convex, in which one side is like the magnifying glass and the other is flat (*see diagrams*). The plano-convex design is more popular as it avoids some of the problems associated with double-convex lenses (chromatic aberration being the biggest). These lenses tend to be put into a housing that protects them from scratches as well as "stray light." Most housings tend to be black, because light entering the scope that isn't coming straight into the lens is of no interest to us and actually can obscure what we are trying to see. Most scope lenses are "coated" meaning they have had a number of very thin layers of chemicals deposited on them that eliminate most of the remaining stray light problems. The best scopes, in my opinion of course, have coated lenses and opaque (black) housings.

The Magnification Follies We use scopes because they magnify our targets, make them bigger in our view, so how much magnification should we use? My best answer is "as much as you can handle." (Hint: Not much.) The problem with magnification is the higher it is, the more of your own movement will be magnified. If you can only see the X-ring in a target face, a very tiny movement of your bow and scope will result in the X-ring no longer being visible. This "apparent movement" of the image in your scope affects all kinds of things. If you can't get the movement down to a small amount you will be shooting on the fly, shot after shot. These movements lead you to believe you are not steady enough and will undermine your confidence, etc. When it comes to magnification, less is more.

How Much, For Pete's Sake? I will start by telling you that 4X, 3X, and 2X scopes are the most popular and a lot of archers will use a 6X scope indoors where there is no wind and constant lighting. Does that help? It shouldn't because there are no such things as "two power" and "four power" scopes.

Think about it. Magnifying lenses work by converging light from the object to a smaller and smaller space. I am sure, if you are male, you remember burning things by using a magnifying lens and focusing sunlight on leaves and twigs (and ants). Archery scopes are like those magnifying glasses but with very long focal point distances. This means the farther you get from the scope, the greater the magnification and the closer the lens the less. Well, how much is there at my draw length, for example?

Consider a 1.0 diopter scope lens. What's a diopter? The diopter value of a lens is the focal length in meters divided into the number 1. It is a kind of physical measure of magnifying power. A 1.0 diopter lens, therefore has a focal length of one meter (39.37 inches), well beyond the usual distance of scope to eye. This might also be labeled an 8X lens using a quite *incorrect* formula that M = 8D or "magnification equals the number of diopters times 8." Let's see how distance from scope to eye affects the "power" of this lens. Since a typical distance from eye to scope is about 35″, the magnification comes out to be about 9.0, so that's close. What about longer? How about 40″? Since that distance is beyond the focal point of the lens, the image flips over and booga booga. I picked a 1.0 diopter lens to illustrate this fact. You can also see that a simple scope is limited to about this power unless your draw length is quite long (creating a short eye to scope distance).

Okay, how about shorter distances? At 30″ from eye to scope the 1.0 diopter lens comes in at about 4.9 power. But, that isn't anywhere near 8X! At 25″ we are looking at under 3X. I hope now you can see that the power of a scope lens is strongly determined by your draw length in the form of the eye-to-scope distance. The "magnifications" listed on the package are at some specified distance (not included on the packaging by the way) just like draw weights of recurve bows are determined at a particular draw length.

If you like math, here's the scope magnification formula:

$$M = 1/(1-d*D)$$

where:

M = Magnification

d = distance from eye to lens in meters

D = Diopter value of the lens

Mathews Archery did us all a favor by creating a nomograph of this relationship. By lining up any straight edge on the diopter vale and eye-to-scope distance you can just read the magnification off of the scale (*see next page*). Really any two of the three allows you to read off the third. Way cool.

Peep Sights: What Do They Do?

I don't know who came up with the idea of the peep sight, but it was brilliant. Instead of having to learn how to sight along side a very blurry bowstring (the danged thing is almost in your eye, so there is no way to focus on it), a peep sight is a lozenge with a hole in it that when inserted into the string allows you to look right through the string. Not only that but they improve your vision at the same time!

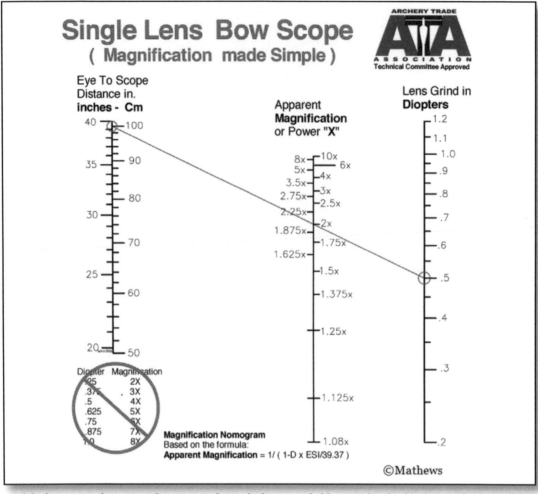

Single Lens Bow Scope
(Magnification made Simple)

ARCHERY TRADE
ATA
A S S O C I A T I O N
Technical Committee Approved

Eye To Scope
Distance in.
inches - Cm

Apparent
Magnification
or Power **"X"**

Lens Grind in
Diopters

Magnification Nomogram
Based on the formula:
Apparent Magnification = 1/ (1-D x ESI/39.37)

©Mathews

Luckily for you, Mathews created a nomograph on which you can hold a straight edge lined up on the diopter value of your lens and the distance from eye to lens and read off the real power you are getting. You should be able to find acopy of this on the Internet. Thanks, Mathews!

The peep has to be manufactured so that there is a round hole in front of your eye at full draw. But the bowstring is at a steep angle in that position so the hole was made on a 45° angle so that it would be horizontal when the string was at that angle. (The advent of shorter and shorter compound bows has lead to another peep being required (a 37° peep) to deal with the more acute string angles these bows have).

Peep Sights Improve Your Vision People can take off their glasses and shoot fairly well if they have a peep sight. (But we still can't see our danged scorecards, so many of us still shoot in our glasses rather than to have to put them on and take them off all of the time.) The reason for this small miracle is that the small hole in the peep only allows light to pass through part of your aiming eye's lens (usually the center). It is defects and distortions of our lenses that create our vision problems. When you see an optometrist for an eye exam, they may give you a paddle with holes in it to look through. Usually one of those holes is small enough to find a near perfect section of your lens and you'll have clear vision.

That's the good part. The not-so-good part is that to do that they have to reduce the amount of light getting into your eye, so peeps reduce the brightness of the image, too. Now, if you are out on a bright sunny target field there is probably no problem, but many field ranges take you from shooting positions that are in full sun to those that are in deep shade. The hardest is when you are shooting from bright sun into deep shade. The bright sun where you are standing causes your irises to get quite small and then the peep reduces the amount of light even more, but the target is in deep shade so it isn't reflecting much light at all. (I have been in cases where we ended up shooting "by Braille," that is we'd get an initial line up looking around the peep and then swing the peep into place and shoot, while seeing nothing of the target at all. Another solution is for another archer to hold up a hat or something to give you artificial shade for your aiming eye.)

Peep technique involves having the edge of the hole of the peep aligned around the outside edge of a circular target (or one of the circular rings). The apparent size of the hole can be adjusted by choosing peeps with different-sized holes and by moving the aperture in and out on the sight's extension bar.

One way to *not* do this is to "drill out" the existing hole to make a peep with a larger hole. The edge of the hole needs to be sharp so that it appears perfectly round at a range of angles it makes with your eye. Drilling leaves a tube down the middle of the peep, which will change apparent shape with angle of view. Don't be cheap; buy another peep with the right-sized hole. (Okay, yeah, I did it too, until I learned better.)

Peeps with Magnification Some peep sights come with little lenses in them. These tend to be problematic in fog or rain as they collect water and obstruct vision (a peep with a hole in it can be blown free of water) so many will only use them indoors. These beasties come with various catchy names: clarifiers, verifiers, magnifiers, etc. My only recommendation is that you be aware that all of these have trade-offs: some make the target more clear and the aperture less clear, some make the entire image clearer but reduce the magnification, etc. Let the buyer beware! (Our motto is "always try before you buy.")

Vision Correction

There is so much more to be said about this topic but this chapter is already overlong, so I will just include a little something about vision correction.

If your vision is anything less than 20:20, you may need vision correction. For archery, there is a hierarchy. If you get by with no correction, that is best. If you can get laser-corrected vision (Lasik, etc.) that is next best. After that comes contact lenses, and dragging up the rear is corrective eyeglasses. Each of these has their plusses and minuses; the eye glasses being just the final option when none of the other solutions are available.

If you are, like me, stuck in eye glasses (I have the worst case vision for an archer—off-axis astigmatism.) consider getting quality shooting glasses. Mine rest snug against my face and have very small bifocal dots at the bottom so I can see my score card. They were well worth the money.

Additional Learning References

Aiming to Win by Bob Ryder (AFm, Vol 18, No 2)
Aiming Better by Larry Wise (AFm, Vol 17, No 4)
Why Shooting Glasses by Chuck Cooley (AFm, Vol 11, No 3)
Shooting in Glasses by Chuck Cooley (AFm, Vol 11, No 5)
What You See is What You Hit by Anthony Hall (AFm, Vol 10, No 2)
The Aperture: Signpost of the Shot by George Tekmitchov (AFm, Vol 3, No 5)

Coach Kim H.T. of Korea was the coach who convinced me that the finger release was teachable, so the least I can do is show you what he looks like.
(Photo Courtesy of Andy Macdonald)

Still More on Coaching Archery

Chapter 23
Teaching the Finger Release

Most of us learned archery with our fingers on the string. Some of us still shoot that way. Since the loosing of the string is basically a nonevent, can we teach our students "how" to release the string? Should we?

Words, Words, Words

Since the finger loose of the string is such a subtle thing, my feeling is that one needs to teach it through multiple channels. One of those channels is a verbal description of what it is we want. The key points are: the string hand must be relaxed (the muscles making the "hook" being in the upper forearm, not in the hand) and one doesn't "try" to "let go" of the string. (As Don Rabska says, "Let the string go, don't let go of the string.")

Obviously words alone won't do it, so there are some physical guides, too. I ask my archers to hold their upper string forearm as they make a number of string hooks in succession. By doing this they can feel those forearm muscles flexing. I then ask them to make a hook with their hand out in front of them. I then match their hook while facing them and link the two together. I then direct them: "don't lose your hook" while I pull and gently shake their hand and arm back and forth, also saying "relax, relax." You can feel the tension leaving their arm as you do this. Their arm should become rubbery all the way up to their shoulder. (This proves that a relaxed arm and a firm hook are compatible.)

This latter drill can be extended into a game. Two facing archers connect their hooks like this and see which can release their hook faster than the other. Most archers will soon realize that if they tense their hands, they lose. The finger loose has to be, well, loose.

Another Drill

I use grocery store plastic bags (the flimsy ones with the handles) as a training aid. I stick 1-2 water bottles into the bag and then ask students to hang the bag at their side. The handle "straps" are rolled up to simulate a bowstring, and the "string" has to be in position in a proper hook. I then ask them to play with it a little: have them see if they can notice a stretching feeling in their hand. Have them tense their hand. Have them relax it. Try to feel the "stretch" when relaxed. (They need to know the difference in feel between a tense hand and a relaxed one; you are not asking them to practice tensing their string hand.)

After they have played with this rig for a minute or two, ask them to see if they can get the bag to drop without moving their fingers. This will perplex some in that they do not distinguish between them moving their fingers to get it to drop from allowing the gravitational pull on the bag to push/move their relaxed fingers out of the way, but I have yet to meet anyone who couldn't achieve this with some practice.

Alternatives are using a small plastic bucket with a wire bale and a couple of large stones in it. With this particular drill setup a bit more feedback can be teased out. If you get off of the "string" (the bale) cleanly the bucket will fall flat and hit a hard floor with a resounding bang. If you roll the release or release in any way sloppily, the bucket will land on one edge before the rest and you get a very different sound. Do avoid dropping it on your feet!)

More Drills

Shooting blind bale with a low draw weight bow can really allow an archer to zero in on the feel of relaxing the bow fingers. Because the tension on the hook caused by this very light bow (ca. 10 pounds) is so low, only very rapid relaxing of the string fingers will result in the arrow leaving cleanly. Arrows leaving straight into the target will make a solid "whap!" sound with very little residual vibration. Arrows leaving at an angle due to a slop-

py release will make less sound initially and more vibration thereafter.

Another drill I learned from Coach Kim H.T. of Korea. The student is set up with a low draw weight bow with the coach in Position One (face-to-face). The archer is asked to go to full-draw-position and the coach holds the riser below the grip and the archer's wrist behind their string hand. The coach counts 1-2-3 and then pulls the hand back toward the elbow. The archer focuses on relaxing the string fingers. Obviously explaining what will happen first is a very good idea. Also, it is important for the archer to link the rearward travel of string hand and elbow to the use of her own back muscles (in

Coach Kim H.T. of Korea (back to camera) was the first coach to demonstrate to me a technique for teaching the finger release. He convinced me that it is "teachable."

this drill simulated by the coach). The archer in the drill is focused on the relaxation of the fingers and the movement of the string hand (straight back, several inches). When they try it on their own, if their string hand doesn't move back, they are not using their back muscles correctly.

Conclusion

There are many aspects of the finger loose (I would argue most) that take care of themselves if the archer simply adopts correct full-draw-position using the correct back muscles. But other aspects are amenable to training. As with all other facets of training form and execution, the shot is broken down into small parts to help the archer to concentrate on what is happening during that part. Since all of the "feel" is internal, putting them into positions in which they can focus upon that "feel" can help them acquire the necessary skills.

Additional Learning References

Drilling for Archery by Steve Ruis (AFm, Vol 14, No 5)
Is the Dead Release Really Dead? by Steve Ruis (AFm, Vol 7, No 2)
Developing the Magic Release by Don Rabska (AFm, Vol 6, No 2)

Wouldn't it be nice if, in our coach training courses, they would describe ways to get archers from where they are to optimal form, instead of just describing optimal form and leaving it up to us to figure out how to get our students there?

Chapter 24
Getting from "Here" to "There": We Need the Pathways . . . Now!

I wrote this just after I finished up facilitating a Level 3 Coach training course taught by Larry Wise. One thing Larry and I were in absolute agreement on was that the course only taught (as they all do) what an elite recurve or compound archer would be doing, in other words, the course describes the ideal goal, the place or the "there" to which we were to guide our students. We were also in agreement that the pathways taking students from where they are ("here") to where we want them to be ("there") have not yet been described. They are needed. They were needed yesterday. What we are doing now is telling our coaches: "That is where we want them to be; you figure out how to get your students there."

That's asking a lot from a volunteer coach.

Let's take a look at this.

What Others Do

We Americans aren't particularly good at mining what we can learn from others. We seem to think that because we are "leaders" we will figure out what to do and others will follow our lead. About the only time we are open to carefully studying others is when somebody up and kicks our ass, which the Koreans (particularly the women) did starting in the 1980s in Olympic Recurve archery and continue to do today. (If you look at the World Archery Record book, I think you will find that Korean record holders outnumber all of the other countries combined.)

Who was #1 before the Koreans? We were. How did the Koreans get ahead of us? They studied us and improved on what we were doing. So what have we done? Many archers were curious about what the Koreans were doing that made them so good (I have written about this before) and we were curious enough to study their methods. We even hired a Korean Olympic Archery Coach who developed his teachings based on what he learned in Korea as their head coach.

We haven't done much studying of other countries, so what have we learned about Korea's system? In their system, they start developing elite Olympic Recurve archers at the age of eight basically by asking them to perform exactly as an elite archer would so that after ten years of such practice they are extremely proficient at it.

So, would their system work here? Obviously yes, if you could find parents who want to train their children to be Olympic archery champions no matter what the kids think now or for the next ten years. Of course, American kids have figured out ways to change their parent's minds that probably don't work on Korean parents, but if enough volunteers could be found it probably could be done.

Is our current system set up to do this?

No.

What We Do

In our youth archery programs recreational archers (the majority) are mixed in with the serious archery competitors (a small minority). Are we willing to abandon the recreational archers and just focus on the small minority? I do not think so; I have never seen anyone advocate for this.

So what do we need?

We need a training pathway that will take our archers from where they are ("here") to where we want them to be ("there") in small increments that we can introduce to our students. Over time, some will continue and some will opt out. The ones who opt out will, we hope, become recreational archers who will enjoy our sport for the rest of their lives. We will continue to give them what coaching they want or need; we won't dump them overboard. The others will be fed more and more over time and their performances will separate themselves from the others.

This requires pathways, certainly at least one, from "here" to "there." As a start, since we are breaking the training into form elements and deciding when they are to be introduced, we need to look at the "there" form elements and ask ourselves which ones are better introduced earlier and which ones can be introduced later.

A Beginning on Developing a Pathway to Elite Archery Form

First, we need a starting point and since I have a tough hide I will offer a beginning for you all to shoot holes in.

Examples of Things That Can Be Left Until Later I expect these would be relatively easy to learn; they don't require many preliminary steps, for example, and don't preclude reasonable levels of success. As an opener I offer you "stance." Stances create stable platforms for our upper bodies to function upon. Olympic recurve archers are recommended to adopt a wide open stance (~30° open to a line to target and ~40°-45° open to shoulder line). The torsion created between feet and shoulders makes for a more rigid, steady platform that is better at resisting wind forces, for example. But youths have little core muscle mass and tend to be quite flexible about their vertical axis so there is little to no benefit. This can be left until later, so start with something simple and repeatable that supports accuracy, a square stance, and move on. Other stances can be explored later.

Teaching elite stances is clearly not the first rung on our ladder from "here" to "there."

Another example might be the "hip tuck" taught to Olympic recurve archers. There is little effect on accuracy or consistency and it can be taught effectively and easily later.

The "hip tuck" is also not an early rung on our ladder from "here" to "there."

Examples of Things That Cannot Be Left Until Later I might as well let the cat out of the bag, as the saying goes, in that I believe there is an early form element that is crucial to create and that is "good alignment." Giving archers good form (T-Form) at full draw with their string (*aka* draw) elbows in proper position is a critical element of good performance.

Being out of line is a major source of inaccuracy and inconsistency.

I have many recurve or compound archers come to me for lessons who have been shooting for a quite while. I typically have to get them to relax and reshape their hands, but then the main issue is getting them to shoot with better, at least acceptable, line. I often end up closing their stances because their "taught-by-formula" open stances lead to open hips, which lead to open shoulders that can't get into line. (Closing the stance lengthens the draw, opening it shortens it.) Removing the influence of an incorrect open stance altogether is often all that is needed to get an archer into line. Later they can experiment with other stances, but it will be from a base of shooting with good line.

Teaching shooting with "good line" should be very early on our ladder from "here" to "there."

Another example of critical early elements is relaxed and properly shaped hands. Most coaches will do this during first lessons: get their bow hands properly placed on the bow and relaxed (wrist, too) and getting their string or release hand properly shaped and relaxed. Tension in the hands creates variable draw lengths, release aids that won't go off, and numerous other problems. The tension in the hands leads to tension being acceptable elsewhere. Relaxed hands tend to help keep other muscles relaxed, too.

Teaching shooting with "relaxed and properly shaped and positioned hands" should be very early on our ladder from "here" to "there."

Okay, I Got the Ball Rolling

None of my opinions may survive but this might just be a start and we need to be working on this now (we needed it years ago). We need our professional coaches to chime in as well as our summer camp coaches. We all have a place in this debate.

What are your thoughts?

Additional Learning References

Correcting Poor Shooting Form by Steve Ruis (AFm, Vol 16, No 1)
How to Teach Archery? by Steve Ruis (AFm, Vol 12, No 6)
Where Form Flaws Come From by Steve Ruis (AFm, Vol 11, No 3)
Shooting Form Analysis by Van Webster (AFm, Vol 9, No 6)
Teaching Form by Steve Ruis (AFm, Vol 9, No 5)
A Comparison of Forms by Larry Wise (AFm, Vol 5, No 1)
Good Shooting Form and the Body Geometry Connection by Mike Gerard (AFm, Vol 3, No 2)

One of the ways one can learn to be a better coach is to study case studies, essentially testing yourself. Another way to learn is to eaves drop on good coaches. The photo is of Master Coach M.J. Rogers working with one of my students, Brent Harmon.

Chapter 25
A Coaching Case Study:
What Would You Do?

The Canadian archery folks use case studies to train coaches and judges and I think we should, too. Here's one to consider.

Case Study

A Senior Olympic Recurve archer approached me for lessons. His story was that he had been a fairly good Junior archer but life interposed and he'd had an extended layoff and was just getting back into the sport. To prepare he had gotten new equipment and read many of the extensive "how to shoot" books, but he complained that he was kind of all over the place and could come nowhere near his old form and scores.

In our first session, I verified that he was, indeed, all over the place, so we talked about his old form. For one, he used to shoot with a closed stance, but because of the book recommendations he had adopted an open stance. He had made quite a few other changes, also. I asked him whether he thought he could reconstruct his old shot and he thought he could, so I sent him off to do so.

At our next session, he'd closed his stance and was shooting in a much better style. Further examination, though, showed that he wasn't quite in line and he was turning his chin to get through his clicker. The chin turning was a clicker cheat needed possibly because his clicker was too far in. The lack of line, though, indicated that his clicker was possibly too far out. Too far in? Too far out?

So, what would you do?

What I Recommended

I am not absolutely sure why I reacted the way I did, but here's what I suggested. (And yes, I have a healthy ego, but I do not think this was the best way to handle this situation; it is merely a way.)

I suggested that he close his stance a bit more.

If you find this recommendation perplexing, let me tell you what happened. After a short discussion of what I meant (I prefer closed stances in which the feet are approximately parallel or at least splayed out to the same degree, just with a shoe tip line heading to the right of the target (for right-handed archers), a few shots blank bale showed that his line was now "good" (not great, but his draw elbow was in the same vertical plane as the arrow was).

Next I asked him to start his shot with his chin up, and as I often do when introducing a new form element I asked him to exaggerate it (as there is a tendency to revert back to old form). A dozen or shots later, he seemed to be coming through his clicker in good order, so I asked him to shoot at a target (we were indoors and it was an NFAA indoor face). After emptying his quiver, he had a nice tight group about six inches to the left of the spot and about three inches high. His comment, after appreciating his rare good group, was that he had expected his arrows were a bit stiff. I suggested we check his bow.

With an arrow on his bow, it was clear his aperture was inboard about one-half of an inch. So, we moved it out until it was exactly over the arrow. His next shot went into the spot. (Yes!)

The shot after that was a bit high, but that was to be expected, too.

Still Puzzled?

Here is what each change accomplished.

Change to a More Closed Stance Any archer who is struggling to get "in line" should consider closing their stance, or closing their stance more, as it makes getting in line easier. I know this sounds heretical because so many others are saying you must have an open stance, but if you can't get in line (a major problem) what good is an open stance (a minor benefit)? My approach is to get archers into good line and have them shoot that way until it feels normal. Then, if they want to experiment with different stances it will be from a position where shooting in line is "normal" and to be kept that way.

Raised Chin A raised chin is necessary for a low or Olympic anchor. In a side or high anchor, a lower chin is possible, but with the low anchor, the string must fling the fingers away from their position under the chin. If the chin is down, the jaw line is sloping downward from back to front and the fingers will slide along the jaw line, lowering the anchor position all the while. The chin must be high enough that it is out of the way of the swinging fingers.

Shooting High and Left What happens when you rotate and lower your chin while trying to clear the clicker? Since your head is at an angle, as the chin rotates to the right, it causes left arrows. Lowering the chin causes high arrows. To counter these forces, the sight aperture must be set in to the right and slightly lower than it should be. When you stop moving the chin, the arrows go back to landing high and left. When the aperture is replaced into the same vertical plane as the arrow, the arrows now go down the middle, but since no correction was made to the elevation of the aperture, the arrows will still group a bit high.

Take Aways

So, what can you take away from this case study? What I learned was to trust my instincts more and not to depend on book knowledge so much. If I were following the textbook, so to speak, I might have judged the athlete's initial closing of the stance to be a mistake (we all know an open stance is "better") and backtracked on that, which would have been a mistake.

If you are skeptical of the role a closed stance can playing getting good alignment, consider this. In recurve archer form, the front shoulder is more important than the rear. "What? But all of the attention in the training programs is on the rear shoulder!" you say.

That is true and what isn't emphasized (and should be) is that if the front shoulder is out of position, there is almost nothing that the rear shoulder can do to fix the problem. A closed stance requires the archer to open up their front shoulder to get the arrow pointed at the target. If the upper bow arm isn't in line with the shoulders, the rear cannot, I repeat, cannot get in line with the front shoulder and you will not have good line.

I would love to have someone more knowledgeable than I write an article listing all of the "clicker cheats" there are and the consequences of those behaviors. Until that becomes available, we will just have to analyze each as it is observed.

Also, obviously having a still head is an asset (but not a requirement; see the gyrations of superstar archer Michele Frangilli).

And, I hope I don't sound like I am bragging, but the value of a good coach seems to be underestimated in archery. Here was a good archer, who after a lengthy layoff wanted to get back into it and so looked to instructional books as an aid. All he found were recommendations for . . . what? We all know we are each different from one another and, at the same time, we are very much alike. This means that our differences are subtle. Consequently, I think we need to do a much better job of clarifying whom we are talking about when we make recommendations regarding shooting form. How we teach 11-year-olds has to be different from how we teach elite adults, so why aren't we clarifying the difference more? I don't have an answer for that, but I will try to do this better in the future.

If you have a case study to share with coaches or judges, send me an email; you might get published in *Archery Focus* magazine . . . and get a check.

Additional Learning References

Coaching Wisdom by Steve Ruis (AFm, Vol 15, No 4)
Where Form Flaws Come From by Steve Ruis (AFm, Vol 11, No 3)
On Beginning a Coaching Library by Steve Ruis (AFm, Vol 10, No 4)

Not yet, not yet, . . . , now, hurry, hurry!

　　　　　　　　　　　　　　　　Still More on Coaching Archery

Chapter 26
The Overaiming Meme

Olympic Recurve coaches have a meme that is considered a cardinal sin if you break it: "do not overaim." This admonition permeates the writing of recurve coaches at all levels. The USA Archery Level 2 coach training manual, for example, includes a shot sequence with one of the early steps labeled "not yet aiming." I think this warrants a closer examination.

Aiming

So what constitutes aiming? Is it just the act of aligning a sight aperture with a point of aim? Clearly this is not the case. Aiming starts from the very beginning of the shot cycle when the archer takes a stance. A condition for accuracy is that the arrow must be in a vertical plane going through the target center for it to hit the center (absent wind effects, etc.). When an archer steps onto a shooting line and effects a square stance, you can see that a vertical plane going through the arrow also goes right across the archer's shoe tips. This is why we recommend a square stance to beginners: it is a natural aiming stance, in that by aligning one's shoe tips up with the target center, one is also aligning the arrow up with target center. If you take a square stance and get into reasonable T-Form at full draw, you will be aiming right down the middle. So, aiming begins with the stance.

Later in the cycle the bow gets raised, but how far? What I teach my students is that it needs to be raised to a height such that when the draw is made and the anchor position is found, the sight aperture is naturally centered on the gold (or wherever the archer is aiming). Higher than that or lower than that results in the archer having to move the bow a substantial amount at full draw, a clear waste of time and energy and possibly a use of the wrong muscles. So, raising the bow is an aspect of aiming. (It has been referred to as "pre-aiming" in the past.)

So, is this too much or too soon? Is this overaiming? No. Here's why.

What's Special About Aiming

As an archer moves through her shot sequence, her attention focuses on just one thing, one thing after another, but just one thing at a time. When taking a stance she focuses on just that. When nocking an arrow she focuses on just that. Beginners have to focus more in that they do more consciously, they have to check the index vane, they have to check that the arrow is nocked snuggly under the top nock locator, they have to be sure the arrow is on the rest and under their clicker (if used). This is all done in a trice and without conscious thought by the expert archer, but it is done and all actions are attended to.

So, all through the shot sequence the archer's attention is focused on one and only one thing . . . except during the "aiming" phase. During the aiming phase, the archer must divide her attention between two things: the visual matching of the aperture with target center (or point of aim) and some aspect of her form involved in completing the shot (the draw elbow, tension in the back muscles, etc.).

This is the only step during the shot sequence that the archer's attention gets divided. The admonition to not overaim is not helpful as it violates the coaching dictum of "tell them how to do it right, don't describe how they are doing it wrong." It also is vague and hard to understand. Just what are the characteristics of "overaiming?"

Instead . . .

Instead of this admonition, archers need to learn how to divide their attention during that step.

One simple drill is to have them hold their bow up in an American-style "raise" position. I ask them to focus on the position of the aperture on the target and then switch to focusing on their bow hand, then their bow arm, then their shoulders, etc. all the time keeping their aperture on the target. (You must include rests because the arms get tired holding the bow up.) Just ask them to move their attention and focus around. After just a few minutes of practice, they get pretty good at it. Then ask them to focus on their aperture and without losing that focus, include their bow hand, or their bow arm, or their shoulders, etc. Then ask them to practice doing this (which they can do at home) with the key being able to focus their divided attention on the aperture and their back muscles (some coaches substitute a focus on the draw elbow for the back). Note: My piano teacher taught me this. You can't play different notes with both hands until each hand has learned to play its notes by itself.

Another activity/drill that will enhance an archer's ability to divide their attention is "slow shooting." This is just working through a shot but at a substantially slower pace than normal. Instead of a shot requiring 6-7 seconds, it takes 30-40 seconds done this way. The archer must also focus on what they are supposed to be focusing on. Mindless drills may tone the body but do not sharpen the mind. You must caution them to avoid flitting back and forth between the two tasks (maintain sight picture, finish shot, maintain sight picture, finish shot, etc.).

Another drill might be to ask them to focus only on their aperture position while shooting an end. In the next end they are to only focus only on completing their shot and not at all on their aperture. In the third end they need to divide their attention between their aperture position and finishing their shot. This drill is based on the Goldilocks' Principle: the first end is too much aperture focus, the second end is too much body focus, and the third end is "just right" or at least close to it. Often the third end shows a much better group than either of the other two (as it should).

A Fine Point

When writers do address this topic (almost never directly) they tend to mention visual focus on the aperture, which is correct, and a visualization involving the draw elbow or scapulas as a means of making sure execution of the shot is continuing, which is incorrect. The power of visualizations is that they involve the brain triggering the same muscles that will be used during the activity visualized, so they are great for rehearsals. But the visual cortex is being asked to do two visual tasks in this approach, which has to lead to some confusion. Instead the visual focus on the aperture's position needs to be combined with the tactile sensations in the back or draw arm that can be associated with correct execution.

But . . . Isn't this a Form of "Multi-Tasking?

Recently psychologists have studied "multi-tasking," that is doing two or more tasks at once, and have claimed that this is often not what people think. Instead of two tasks being done simultaneously, the minds of the people doing these tasks were switching back and forth between the two and each task thus suffered in quality. The simultaneity was an illusion. Example tasks were given such as trying to do math problems while listening to a Presidential speech and extracting salient information. I believe they had brain scans to back up their claim. But it is not the case that if this is true some of the time, it is true all of the time.

Arguments by example, how scientists explain complex things to ordinary people like you and me, can be opposed by counter examples, so let me offer a few. About in third grade most American kids are presented with the task of "rubbing their stomach and patting their head" (or is it the reverse?) from a "friend." At first none can do this as it seems impossible. But after a short period of practice, many can do these two different tasks simultaneously (maybe not so well, as practice usual stops when the feat is achieved). Some of these kids may grow up to be a piano player, with each of their hands is doing something different and simultaneous, or maybe a virtuoso rock 'n' roll drummer who can play complex rhythms, sometimes with different meters, simultaneously with both hands and a foot.

To end this argument with a sports metaphor, consider a baseball batter. He might have to track the curved path of a ball thrown from a variety of "release points" at near 100 mph while swinging a baseball bat to intercept that ball to hit it the opposite direction and which are close enough to the batter to cause significant bodily harm were he to be hit by the pitch. If they can do those tasks simultaneously, I think we can do our task simultaneously: our target is not even moving! All it takes is practice.

Please note, I am not refuting or rejecting the psychologists' research. I believe they are absolutely correct when it comes to two simultaneous and complex conscious tasks, but the subconscious mind seems capable of attending to a great many tasks simultaneously.

Conclusion

Perhaps it is time to bury the "overaiming" meme. It was never particularly helpful. It is not an instruction of "what to do" but rather "what not to do." And I don't think it accurately described the issue at hand.

There was a time in the late 60s or early 70s when the clicker was being adopted that a number of archers were using it as a draw check only and would hold for more than several seconds after the clicker "clicked." Many of these archers were taking too much time at full draw and could be described as overaiming, but no one is doing that now.

Coaches inherit too much stuff that has outlived its usefulness and I think this falls in that category.

Additional Learning References

Aiming Better by Larry Wise (AFm, Vol 15, No 5)
Conscious vs. Unconscious Aiming by Rick McKinney (AFm, Vol 6, No 2)

Where to start . . . where to start?

Still More on Coaching Archery

Chapter 27
The Stages of Learning Archery, Part 1

There is so much missing from the archery coach's arsenal. In other sports, procedures for teaching many of their sport-specific procedures have written protocols. And it is not unusual for there to be disputes between coaches about the best way to teach something. I wish this were the case in archery, but it is not. Our coach training programs are almost universally focused on what to coach and, unfortunately not, how to coach. This leaves coaches in the dark about what to teach when as well as how.

As an example, yesterday I was watching a young JOAD archer struggling shot after shot. All of her shots landed on the left side of the target because she had a "floating anchor," that is her anchor position had almost no contact with her face. I asked her coach if he had been the one who introduced her to her clicker, because she was clearly struggling with basic elements of her form and I thought that the clicker introduction was premature. His response was he wouldn't have done it if she hadn't had a bad case of target panic.

So the cure for her target panic was a clicker. Setting aside that a clicker does not cure target panic (it is one of the "cures" bandied about informally, but it is not), her floating anchor was not getting fixed while she was negotiating a relationship with her clicker.

In addition, there are no coaching protocols for introducing clickers and for dealing with target panic, but I suspect that a great many similar difficulties could be avoided by focusing on what is important when teaching new archers.

I want to make it very clear that I do not have "the answer" or "all of the answers" to the questions we face. I do think, however, that as a community of archery coaches, we need to hash out what works and what does not. I am putting in my two-cents worth in the hopes that other coaches will do the same so at some point in the future we will have a list of things that are more likely to work – and a list of things that do not work – for coaches to consult.

What Do Beginning Archers Need to Learn and When

When you first learned to shoot, did you realize that you were "building your shot" at the time? I think none of us thought that, we were just having fun. If we didn't have any fun, how long do you think we would have stuck out flinging arrows? Not long I suspect, I am an example of this.

I got a job as a camp counselor at a summer camp while I was in college. In camp, I tried archery and really took to it. When I got home from that job, I used some of my pay to buy a bow and some arrows. The bow was a 32# recurve (a one-piece Browning with a red back; I still remember it). But I have a 31″-32″ draw length, so that bow was actually too much for me to control. Consequently I would get the bow out, shoot a few arrows and then quit. The bow spent most of its time in my closet. I actually spent more of my time thinking about archery than doing it.

When I turned 40 I was loaned a compound bow, combined with some aluminum arrows I bought, to try again. That bow was turned down to 35# of peak weight, and with the benefit of letoff and my full adult musculature, I was off!

I tell you this story because I think the biggest mistake we make when coaching beginners is with draw weight. An archery aphorism is that the easiest way to prevent good archery form is to be overbowed. The young JOAD archer I mentioned above was overbowed. Even though her limbs were backed out as far as they could be, she still had too much draw weight to deal with and that was probably the source of her target panic: wanting and trying to control a bow that was too difficult for her.

Consequently, I urge you to err on the low side of draw weight when it comes to giving new archers a bow to shoot. I start adult beginners with 10# and 14# bows. Often, because their draw lengths are very short, I will start youths on a 16# bow (to get them 10-12# of weight in hand). Yet I have seen programs where beginners were handed bows that were way beyond their capacity (35-40# @ 28″). I think it is a basic principle that:

Beginners should start with very low draw weight bows.

In addition, younger youths should start with lightweight bows. Hand an adult compound bow, even most of the youth full compound bows, to a youth and ask them to hold it out at arm's length and you will find most cannot, certainly not for much time. I am hopeful that enterprising manufacturers will begin to make compound bows with lightweight risers (polymer over a steel backbone?, carbon composite?) so that youths can learn compound archery more easily. As it is, most young compound archers are being taught to shoot while dropping their bow arms because their bows are too heavy to hold up one armed. Every shot they take is reinforcing a form flaw they will have to break later (if there is a later).

First Things Once a beginner is properly bowed, what is to be learned first? Clearly this is basic archery form focused on good T-Form at full draw. In our programs and coach trainings we recommend strongly that each new beginner is lead through their "first three arrows" by a coach, one-on-one. We walk them through taking a stance, how to hold their bow, how to check their armguard is in the right place, where to nock an arrow, how to draw the string, etc. We are not trying to teach them intellectually, but physically. Our goal is for them to be able to get off shots by themselves in fairly good order. We aren't trying to cloud their experience with terminology (this is a nock locator, that is an arrow rest, not!) nor are we trying to teach them what good form is, we just place them into good archery positioning. For example, one common impulse for beginners is to try to draw the bow with a low draw elbow. We simply use a finger to raise their elbow up just before the draw. In this manner we get them started on the right path.

If after the first three arrows, they seem to be able to shoot independently, we then teach them the whistle system and put them on a shooting line. Archers who don't seem to be ready for the shooting line go off to the side to do "the next three arrows" with a coach.

Once an archer can get into good archery full draw positioning (square stance, bow arm straight, etc.) the next things to focus on are the bow and string hands and the anchor position. These archers are shooting barebow. If they can achieve good T-Form with relaxed bow and string hands and a reasonably tight anchor, they will have addressed and handled what I call "the windage problem." Because the arrow and the target are in sight and the ability to point is hardwired into our brains, if an archer's form includes those basic elements the width of their groups will be minimal. (Because our eyes in our head are left and right and not up and down, we don't get the same benefit regarding elevation.) The tight anchor is required because we cannot see the back end of the arrow, so we must align the string with the pupil of our aiming eye (and the nock is attached to the string right below) so that when we point with the front half of the arrow, we are not mis-aiming by having the back end off of that line.

Remember that beginners almost always are learning with borrowed equipment and therefore their arrows are probably too stiff and will thus tend to fly to the left (for right-handed archers). Only with equipment matched to the archer will their arrows align with the target's center when pointed at the center. This is one big reason why we use larger target faces and shorter shooting distances for beginners.

Once good T-Form (producing "good line") is had and combined with relaxed hands and a tight anchor, archers will tend to group fairly well and with practice will become consistent enough that they can be fitted with their own equipment. As has been stated in Archery Focus magazine quite a few times, only when an archer gets equipment fitted to him or her does the feedback being given by the equipment promote further learning.

And Then . . .

So, now we crank the draw weight up? Actually, no. Now is when we teach our students to shoot "off of the point." This takes care of the "the elevation problem" and will also compensate to some extent for arrows being improperly spined.

All of this can occur within just a few lessons (4-6) and I had one adult learner do this, at least the basics, in one lesson. The key was that he started with a 10# recurve, moved to a 14# recurve (each for about 15-20 minutes) and finally to a 20# recurve and aiming off of the point at 13 yards. I would want this student to shoot this way for a lesson or two more before fitting him for equipment, but amazing progress can be made with light drawing bows.

The key is allowing a student to adopt good form under low levels of stress and get used to those proper postures and behaviors. Adding draw weight is a simple thing when you have good form to build upon. If you do not, too much stress will undermine the form the archer has built and undermine further progress.

Things Beginners Tend to Get Wrong

Beginners tend to do a lot of things wrong due to over thinking (which is part of the reason why we gently lead beginners by means of a series of short instructions). It is common to see young boys take the bow in hand and be completely incapable of drawing the bow. Because in their mind, the task is going to be difficult (note the sound effects in the movies when a bow is drawn; there is always creaking to indicate the strain—kids don't get these ideas from a vacuum), they flex every muscle they've got (they don't know which muscles are required) and are therefore incapable of moving, let alone drawing the bow. When these little boogers finally relax, all is well.

Beginners tend to struggle with a short list of things:

Nocking Arrows Our experience is that nocking arrows is the most difficult step for beginning archers. Allow your students to struggle so they can figure it out. We do insist, though, that they load their bows with the bows vertical. We do not want them to get into the habit of loading their bows sideways as they will be interfering with other archers on future shooting lines. (One of our coaching principles is to teach new archers in such a way to avoid embarrassment in the future. If you bump people on the line at a tournament, they will talk to you and possibly not kindly so. Also, having to learn a new behavior at a tournament is not a recipe for success and smaller things have driven folks out of the sport.)

Tilted Heads After beginners have shot a dozen arrows or so, you will see them tilt their heads so as to look down the arrow shaft as a form of aiming. This happens like clockwork. You can count on it. We reinforce that the head be vertical before the bow is raised and then not moved throughout the remainder of the shot. A single finger can reposition a head tilt at full draw. (Be sure to tell the archer you are going to do this; you don't want any surprises.)

Death Grips The harder a bow is to draw, the harder a beginner squeezes the grip. (Another reason for starting on a light drawing bow.) Obviously squeezing the grip doesn't help you draw the bow. In fact, tension in one hand tends to contribute to tension in the other. Proper bow hand positioning and behavior is not obvious and needs to be taught. Adults tend to want reasons; kids generally just want to be shown.

Conclusion

Giving new archers a good start toward achieving good form and execution is invaluable. It not only increases the likelihood the archer will continue (part of the fun is hitting the target!) but can also prevent problems that will need to be dealt with later.

So, my priorities in launching new archers are:

1. Safety (Always!)

2. Good Basic T-Form

3. Soft/Relaxed Bow and String Hands

4. A Tight Anchor Position

All of these will result in good grouping, which is the signal that:

5. Aiming Off the Point

can be learned. All of this needs to be accomplished with very low drawing bows, as light-weight as practicable.

If archers are to continue, what is in their best interest? I believe it is shooting with good alignment, not a particular stance, or any other thing. Sure other things are important: relaxation, focus, etc. but being used to shooting with their bodies in good line will serve them as a foundation for anything they are to do later. To that end I focus on the above list to encourage them being able to shoot with good alignment and to consider that "normal."

Additional Learning References

Correcting Poor Shooting Form by Steve Ruis (AFm, Vol 16, No 1)
How to Teach Archery? by Steve Ruis (AFm, Vol 12, No 6)
Where Form Flaws Come From by Steve Ruis (AFm, Vol 11, No 3)
Shooting Form Analysis by Van Webster (AFm, Vol 9, No 6)
Teaching Form by Steve Ruis (AFm, Vol 9, No 5)
A Comparison of Forms by Larry Wise (AFm, Vol 5, No 1)

A common transition point for beginning archers is when they go to their first (or second, or third, . . .) competition. Usually, the thought is "Hey, if I practiced I could get really good at this."

Still More on Coaching Archery

Chapter 28
The Stages of Learning Archery, Part 2

In the last chapter I addressed what the stages of learning archery are for beginners, as I saw them (of course). Once a beginner gets through the early stages of learning how to shoot, what comes next? Let's look at this.

Non-newbies and Archery

Once a student has reached a point where they have solid basic form and are shooting off the point (or by any other aiming technique), what are the next "stages" of their learning? I think what comes next are not stages per se but transitions. The order of these does not appear to be fixed.

One transition comes when the archer gets fitted and acquires their own equipment, so that it can be set up for them and tuned. We think that this is the beginning of "intermediate status" for an archer, being the combination of good basic form and owning their own equipment (and having it fitted and having it properly set up). This does not, however, distinguish between recreational and competitive archers.

A relatively minor transition comes when archers attend their first competition: from just participating in "archery classes" or "archery lessons" they move into the wider world of the sport. They get exposed to archers of other styles, ages, attitudes, etc. The exposure to competition may or may not have a significant effect on the archer.

A third transition can occur when the archer makes a more profound commitment to learning the sport. We call archers who have made this commitment "competitive archers" because it is usually only through the effects of competition that true excellence can be pursued. Archers who do not make this commitment we call "recreational archers;" these are archers whose primary goal is "having fun." These two categories of archers necessarily train differently. Recreational archers won't stick with any training drills that are boring because they are "not fun." Competitive archers will do all kinds of things that are "not fun" if they think it will help them perform better. This transition often comes with a beginning-to-intermediate archer being exposed to competition and doing fairly well. They then think something along the lines of "if I worked at this a little harder I could be really good."

You can see the differences in a typical JOAD class. The recreational archers go to JOAD class and the next time they practice is . . . the next JOAD class. The competitive archers are practicing on several days between JOAD classes. There are, of course, other differences.

A Coach's Role in these Transitions

Recently I saw one of my students, who is a JOAD coach, get large numbers of his students to show up for a FITA Field tournament (in fact there were more kids than adults!). For many of these youths, this was their first tournament. He did this by: inviting his students, preparing them to go by providing information to both the archers and their parents, and also by making sure the students had enough sight marks to shoot the shoot. In addition he provided for a set of "novice stakes" at each target (at unchanging distances) so the brand-new students had a chance of shooting a decent score.

So, do you think coaches have a role to play in helping students through these transitions? The obvious answer is yes.

Going to a First Competition The example above is just one of hundreds of actions that archery coaches take to get their students to their first competition. Anything you can do to make that first competition feel ordinary is considered good preparation. It may include staging a mock competition (some do this with timers and lights, etc.). I tend to think the best place to start is with an indoor competition in that it is climate-controlled, with no wind, you don't have to worry about rain or lightning or bugs, etc. I now think I was wrong, after seeing those kids have a blast on a difficult field course (a two-day event, with one day unmarked yardages, the other marked, but longer) that involved some rain.

Having the tournament close by is good. Other than that, encouragement and preparation covers a lot of bases.

Be aware that something doesn't necessarily click at the first tournament, sometimes it is at the second or third. And sometimes it doesn't happen at all, but if they don't go to the first, it can't happen there or at the second, etc.

Getting Fitted Transition We think this is so important that we created a "bow fitting" course for beginning coaches. In that course we teach basic bow fitting (bow length, draw weights, draw lengths, costs, everything) and we teach basic arrow fitting (spine charts, shaft lengths, point weights, fletching, nock fit, everything basic). We felt the need for this because coaches of beginners are often asked for equipment recommendations and some of our coaches are not experienced archers (and the compound people don't necessarily know much about recurve bows and vice versa). We hope to have this course available online soon.

Kids and adults think archery equipment is cool but are clueless as to what to buy and how to set it up. If you aren't already somewhat expert at making such equipment recommendations, educate yourself. A poor equipment recommendation can undermine your coaching reputation quicker than almost anything else.

If you are somewhat expert, you can acquire some student-appropriate used equipment and provide it to your students. I do this with bows and bow sights and provide them to my students to "try" (including some release aids and stabilizers) and will sell them those bows and sights at my cost. I don't make any money on these transactions (other than the lesson fees helping to set up and tune the new equipment); s'all part of the service.

If you are lucky enough to have a good local pro shop, it can't hurt to go over and introduce yourself. They may work with you by carrying some inventory for your students (if you can provide enough sales). If you use bow fitting forms, you may want to familiarize the shop with the forms or you may want to let them do their own thing and then have your students be able to compare your fitting recommendations with the shop's. I try to always explain that shops can have "specials" of which I am not aware that they may want to take advantage of. I also warn them that shops have, in the past, sold inappropriate gear to customers, so if there is a major difference between what the shop wants to sell them and what I have recommended I suggest that they delay buying until they can get more information.

Becoming a Competitive Archer This is a transition that you can be receptive to, but I don't think you can push. We created a JOAD program when we were in California and it grew to the point that we spun off a "team" from the regular classes. This team was for archers wanting to attend competitions and to learn how to win, virtually the definition of a being a "competitive archer." But several of the team members were really recreational archers and were there for the social aspects as much as anything else. No amount of urging, encouraging, requiring, you name it will convert a recreational archer into a competitive one. It has to come from within.

I remember one young man who got a few private lessons from me (with permission from his coach, who was somewhat frustrated with the young man's lack of effort). That young man won a state championship shortly thereafter, but was really a recreational archer. If it weren't for the camaraderie and interaction with his teammates, he'd have switched to another activity in short order.

There is nothing wrong with being a recreational archer! I am one. We all become one, no matter how competitive we were, when we "age out." What you want to do is to be able to recognize the symptoms and treat each student-archer accordingly. If you suspect an archer to be making that transition, slowly add drills or physical training exercises or mental training exercises that are, well not "no fun," but maybe "not much fun" and see if they embrace the tasks. If they do, then it is time for serious planning and serious training.

Additional Learning References
The Elements of Winning Archery by Steve Ruis (AFm, Vol 15, No 3)
Drilling for Archery by Steve Ruis (AFm, Vol 14, No 5)
The Bow Fitting by Steve Ruis (AFm, Vol 12, No 2)
An Intermediate Fitness Plan by Annette M. Musta (AFm, Vol 7, No 4)

If you don't know where to start teaching the mental game, educate yourself. A good place to start that is with "With Winning in Mind" by Lanny Bassham.
(Photo Courtesy of Bob Ryder)

Chapter 29
The Stages of Learning Archery, Part 3

In the first two chapters on this topic I addressed what the stages of learning archery are for beginners, and the accompanying transitions that occur after those early stages. So, if a beginner gets through the early stages of learning how to shoot, then gets their own gear, gets battle tested in competition and makes a commitment to doing some serious training, is there anything archers have in common thereafter? I think so; let's see if you agree.

From Intermediate Archer To. . . ?

Once an archer has her own equipment and has it fitted to her and maybe has done some simple tuning, her equipment then gives her good feedback. What happens next depends on many variables that do not come in any particular order, but that generally involve stages of development. Here are two in particular.

Embracing the Mental Game When (or even whether) an archer embraces the mental game depends on a great many factors: gender (yes, I do think males and females think differently), age, whether the archer is being coached, etc.

It is frequently the case that adult males who come to the sport have a tendency to think that the effort is largely, if not totally, physical. After achieving some physical mastery over their equipment, yet still not placing as high in competitions as they would like, they are apt to concede that "maybe there is something to that mental hoodoo after all." Even when being coached, men tend to resist the mental game more than women. Obviously I have only observed what I have observed and that is a small set of archers. So, take this observation with a grain of salt.

The mental game is an asset for both recreational and competitive archers. Basically, as things are learned they are woven into the archer's shot cycle and then get practiced on a regular basis.

Keep in mind that the mental side of archery (or any other sport for that matter) didn't get much attention until the 1970s. There were a few stalwart coaches beating the drum (I am thinking of Len Cardinale) but their influence was fairly local. At that point in time the mental side of sports was barely visible.

How You Can Help You do not have to overtly announce that you are going to begin "mental training." Instead, I start in the first couple of lessons by introducing the concept of a shot sequence. It creates a terminology that is necessary for further discussion (What's an "anchor," Coach?) but also eventually forms a structural basis for the archer's mental program, although they don't need to know that right away.

When your archer displays poor mental skills, you can address them as they come up. The first such topic to come up is typically "self-talk." Self-talk is what you say to yourself about yourself; it is not just random muttering. Similarly, when an archer working with you says something in frustration, "I'll never be any good!" you can use it as an opportunity to introduce affirmations. Have a good story available as "stories teach." I use the story of Billy Mills' Olympic Gold Medal performance as my teaching tool. (If you don't know the story, look it up; I heard it from the man himself and it was a powerful message.)

These tools can help recreational archers as well as competitive ones, so start early and keep teaching.

Embracing Serious Planning and Serious Training This stage is a bit more nebulous and has a great deal, I believe, to do with the archer's personality. Obviously recreational archers aren't into planning other than maybe for their next tournament attendance, but competitive archers will benefit from even a small amount of time planning, especially when it comes to practice planning.

Planning really should start with practice planning, but never look a gift horse in the mouth. Any planning should be seen as a sign your archer is serious about archery. Practice planning basically means they have an idea of what they want to accomplish in each and every particular practice session. These plans, of course, should be written down and checked off as they are accomplished, so here the archer's notebook comes into play.

We're not suggesting elaborate plans here, just lists of things to do and how to do them. An example might be "bare shaft tuning out to 50m" or "spend 10 minutes with release and rope bow then 10 minutes shooting blind bale." Tasks such as equipment installation, sighting in, tuning, anything that pops up during "practice" should show up on a session's list. These plans (dated and with notations about weather, mood, etc.) collectively become a list of "what happened" and "when" if you need to go back to see if anything has been left out.

How You Can Help I get the ground ready for this by asking each of my archers, competitive or recreational, to make two lists after each tournament they attend: one of those has the heading "Things I Learned" and the other has the title "Things I Will Do Differently Next Time." Each list must have a minimum of three things on it, but more is better.

The best place to make these lists is in their notebook. (I am real subtle. I buy notebooks in bulk cheap and give them away to my students.) I tend to recommend inexpensive spiral-bound school notebooks but anything will do. The key is that after a tournament experience the archer is thinking about what they learned. If something shows up more than once on a "Learned" list, maybe it didn't actually get learned! And the "Things I Will Do Differently Next Time" list informs future practice sessions and tournament preparation. Ask your archer to combine such lists from their last five tournaments and see what they can see. We hope they will see considerable progress and recognize it as such, but if things keep popping up, a "to do" list is automatically suggested.

You can help your archers turn such observations into practice plans. Maybe they have been fighting their clicker or punching their release, so schedule some time to work on that. Maybe they have gotten tense when they realized they were in the hunt for an award. That should be addressed, too. Your archers will look to you for advice as to how to address these issues.

Conclusion

All archers are unique and they are all the same. There are some commonalities in how they get to where they are going. If any of these stages or transitions is skipped, it generally tends to rear up and bite your archer, typically when it is most important that nothing go wrong.

Being aware of these allows you to point out such omissions, in your own fashion (subtle, unsubtle, etc.). If your archer chooses to ignore your advice, well, it is an individual sport. If you fail to bring up something important, maybe no one else will notice, but you should.

Additional Learning References

Mental Rehearsal by Troy Bassham (AFm, Vol 12, No 4)
Running a Mental Program by Troy Bassham (AFm, Vol 11, No 5)
Mental Consistency by Lanny Bassham (AFm, Vol 9, No 6)
Mental Rehearsal by Troy Bassham (AFm, Vol 12, No 4)
Do You Expect to Win? by Steve Ruis (AFm, Vol 14, No 2)

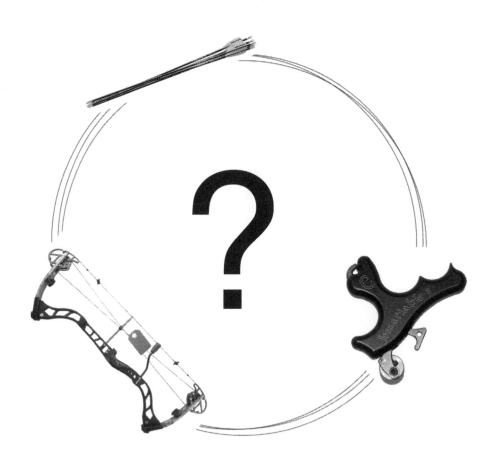

Equipment choices are bewildering to the uninitiated.

Still More on Coaching Archery

Chapter 30
The Stages of Learning Archery, Part 4

We are now addressing how we should approach the beginning stages of training a serious (probably young) archer. In the previous three chapters I addressed dealing with rank beginners, and then the transitions and stages they go through thereafter. In this chapter I will discuss equipment issues, that is, what aspects of archers' equipment are quite important and which are less important.

Obviously, the color scheme an archer prefers in his or her equipment can be designated a low priority, but I am not sure it needs to stay there. I have often pointed out that in compound circles when someone mentions they are going to acquire a new bow they generally start with the manufacturer and model but the very next thing they mention is . . . the color of the bow! (I have done this a time or two myself.) Obviously the color of the bow has no impact on its performance, so why might the color be a factor? I believe it "colors" our appreciation for it. A bow that is a pleasing color appears to us to be closer to our definition of a "good bow" than one that is the "wrong" color. I remember a compound bow that was put out (by a manufacturer I won't name but it rhymes with PSE) that looked like it had been painted by The Grateful Dead; everyone commented upon its appearance and often made up scatological names for the color scheme, things like "Cosmic Vomit." Now, if you are someone who likes attention, the more the better, this may be a plus. If you are someone who wants to stay "under the radar" this would be a definite minus.

In any case, we will focus on the substantive factors in choosing equipment for serious intermediate archers and avoid the merely psychological. Here I am going to focus on only the critical elements: bows, arrows, tabs and releases.

An Underlying Issue

All of what follows must be taken in context. For families and individuals "of means" archery purchases are a small matter. For families and individuals who are struggling financially such purchases can be a bone of contention and can create strife. Coaches need to pay close attention to this issue and not just issue ultimatums about supporting the athlete in the family. As a general practice I tend to have a small supply of older top-of-the-line equipment on hand that I will sell to families at my cost (they are paying me to help their archer explore the equipment and set it up and tune it; that is enough for me). This equipment is of higher quality and lower cost than most new lower-end purchases (although I am finding it harder to find real bargains on older bows as time goes by).

Critical Elements of Serious Beginners' Bows
Let's break this down to Recurve and Compound bows as their criteria are somewhat different.

Recurve Bows Young or up-and-coming adult recurve archers always want a cool-looking bow. Something about having all the "bells and whistles" says "I am recognized as a good archer" and I think this is quite normal. Where this can get in the way of making progress is when the bow is too much to handle. This can come in the form of too much draw weight, the bow being too massive, or the bow requiring greater skill than the archer possesses to be shot well.

Too Much Draw Weight Much has already be written about this and how being "overbowed" is the greatest form killer we know.

Too Much Bow Mass This happens mostly to young archers who rush into a bow with a metal riser, one considerably heavier than their former bow. But often these growing archers do not have enough upper arm development to hold those heavier bows up through the shot so they get months of practice "dropping their bow arms"—something we do not want practiced. The limbs are way more important than the riser. Make sure your young archers have a good reason and the musculature for moving to a heavier bow.

Too Much Skill Required One of our *Archery Focus* authors wrote about how, as an advanced intermediate archer, he received a suggestion from an engineer who worked for his bow's manufacturer that the limbs he had bought required more skill than he possessed and he would be better off with a less exacting set. He changed to less expensive limbs and saw his archery improve and become less frustrating because of it.

Parents of children who are financially well off, often want their children to have "the best" equipment available, which they equate with the "most expensive." This is not always a productive thing to do.

Compound Bows Beginning compound archers often learn on a "zero letoff" bow and want to get into a "real" compound bow ASAP. I think this is also quite normal. What can go wrong with this and can get in the way of making progress is when the bow is too much to handle. This can come primarily in the form of too much draw weight and the bow being too massive. Another problem is that the bow's draw length must be adjusted to the archer's draw length and, if the archer is still growing, this must be attended to . . . frequently.

Too Much Draw Weight Like for recurve bows, much has already be written about how being "overbowed" is the greatest form killer we know. This is complicated by larger letoffs available on many compound bows: "Sure it is a 70# bow, but at 80% letoff, I am only holding 14#!" Yes, the holding weight is low and is easily managed but getting "over the hump," that is to peak weight and down into the "valley," is a thrill ride. Realize that it takes a recurve archer all the way from brace to full draw to hit peak draw weight. Compound archers, who often have higher peak bow weights, get to that weight in two thirds of the distance (the remaining third has the weight dropping from peak to holding weights). This means you have to pull both harder and faster than in a recurve bow. You only need to look around at the large numbers of compound archers weirdly muscling their bows into full draw position by holding them overhead, pointing them downward, etc. to realize the folly of doing this. Your student needs to be able to pull the bowstring smoothly and strongly with the arrow level. If they can't they are overbowed . . . turn it down, even better: start lower!

Too Much Bow Mass For young archers, even the beginner compounds are often too heavy. When they graduate to a "real" compound bow, the bow's mass tends to be even greater—sometimes much greater. As a test, I ask young compound archers to hold their bow up, one armed, in full draw position while I count (slowly). If I don't make it to 5 before their arm starts to drop, that bow is probably too heavy. If they can make it past 8, they are probably okay.

If they are stuck with a too-heavy bow and they are motivated, they need to be doing some physical training (primarily side arm raises with hand weights—a plastic milk jug with water in it (one pint weighs one pound) will do) to build up their deltoid muscles.

Critical Elements of Serious Beginners' Arrows

There seems to be a dichotomy developing in the minds of archers and coaches, and that is aluminum arrows are "okay" but carbon arrows are "better/best." This is nonsensical at best, idiotic at worst (the "carbon is like bacon: it makes everything better" syndrome).

The key elements in a set of competition arrows is that they be straight, equal in length and mass and configuration (FOC and fletching). Tuning is the process whereby we make our arrows most forgiving of our shooting irregularities.

Major Problems For light-drawing youths, the biggest problem is getting a spine match. We see so many young recurve archers with very long arrows and their clickers way out on their sight's extension bar. Similarly compound archers are seen with 6-8 inches of arrow sticking out in front of their bows. Ideally these young archers would have high spine arrows (whippy) that can be cut to a reasonable length for them to shoot. Please realize that I am a big fan of youths cutting their arrows on the long side to allow for their growth and for some shortening as their draw weights go up. But having a foot of arrow sticking out in front of the bow is an impediment to accurate shooting.

The real advantage of aluminum arrows for young archers is the ability to buy a new set when needed for not much money. Easton Jazz and Platinum Plus shafts are quite affordable and come in fairly high spines for short-drawing youths. A dozen can be replaced for less than US$100. Young archers can also learn arrow maintenance on these shafts, when making a mistake is not so expensive.

Now aluminum arrows do have a drawback: they do bend. Straightening them accurately requires an expensive jig or paying a technician at a pro shop to do it for you. Carbon arrows don't bend. They have that advantage. They do crack, though, and when they break they can make spectacularly sharp shards that are quite dangerous. They also cannot be repaired when cracked and are quite a bit more expensive to replace. The vast majority of young archers making the switch from aluminum to carbon see no particular benefit from doing so. But they do look cool.

Where young archers can benefit significantly from all-carbon arrows is when they struggle to "make distance." All-carbon arrows are significantly lighter than their aluminum counterparts, so they provide more cast and can help keep a young archer in reasonable shooting posture during this phase.

Critical Elements of Serious Beginners' Tabs and Releases

There are critical elements of both tabs (for finger shooters) and release aids (for compound-release archers).

Tabs I see a great many young archers jumping almost immediately to a metal frame tab. These tabs are rarely properly sized as most are designed for adults, so these young aspiring archers are trying to shoot while having a bulky thing clutched in their string hand and it shows.

If such tabs can be properly fitted, they are fine. I still prefer a soft tab, like the Wilson Brothers *Black Widow*, that comes in a wide variety of sizes (from XS to XL). They are soft, with a Velcro strap to hold them tight to the hand and allow the hand to shape itself to the jaw line or face. Since it isn't rigid or bulky, it allows the archer to focus on the skin-to-skin contact that is needed for a successful anchor position. They also cost half or less of what the metal frame tabs cost, so for the same price as one metal frame tab, you can buy two *Black Widows*. The student-archers learn to alternate their tabs so they have a broken-in replacement should one get lost, broken, or soaking wet in a rain.

Also, the leathers on most metal-framed tabs are designed for heavier weight bows with higher string pressures, so are thicker and less responsive than these young archers need.

Release Aids I see a plethora of problems surrounding young release shooters. Most issues evolve from poor training, which is not the point of this segment, so instead I will talk about two real equipment issues: release aid size and triggering mechanisms.

Release Aid Sizes I remember encountering a rather good young release shooter in a JOAD class and I commented to both the archer and his parents that his release aid was too large for his hand. They both responded that the model chosen was the "small size" and was fitted at a pro shop. Now I have a lot of respect for what a good pro shop can do for you. I also respect what a poor pro shop can do to you, so the release having been "fitted at a pro shop" didn't say much of anything to me. Basically they were saying "Are you going to believe the size stamped on this thing or your lying eyes, huh?" This young archer's fingers were splayed out much too much and his trigger was not positioned carefully. The release was clearly too big.

The problem here is that very, very few releases are made with kids in mind—small-handed adults, yes . . . kids, no.

A release aid must fit into the draw hand comfortably when that hand is relaxed. If there is a trigger, it must be movable to a place not under the control of a finger- or thumb-tip. End of story.

Release Aid Triggering Mechanisms Since I just mentioned the young release archer above, I might as well mention that the model of release chosen was one that required quite exacting execution to function repeatably. This was highlighted by an Internet debate on that topic that went on for many months and finally was decided by a series of articles published in *Archery Focus* magazine (thanks to Tom Dorigatti). Those articles were based on experiments that explained how and why they were, well, exacting (finicky, really). This was not a release aid I would have recommended to a youth, no matter how accomplished.

There are a great many triggering mechanisms available: triggers that involve the thumb (very popular) and the index finger (popular among bow hunters) and the pinkie finger (not particularly popular). There are also models that have no trigger at all (see below).

Release Aids with Thumb Triggers These are very popular with target archers. The key thing is they have to fit and the part of the thumb the trigger needs to touch is just below the pad.

Release Aids with Index Finger Triggers These are very popular with bow hunter archers, primarily because the triggering mechanism is attached to a band that attaches securely to a wrist band so they cannot be dropped. While you will see some target archers with releases like this. it is generally because these releases cost only a fraction of what the hand-held releases cost. The key thing is they have to fit, meaning a snug but not too tight wrist band, and the part of the index finger the trigger needs to touch is just below the pad of the finger. The bow is drawn with the index finger tucked behind the trigger to avoid premature releases.

Release Aids with Pinkie Triggers These are not very popular with target archers. The key thing is they have to fit and the part of the pinkie the trigger needs to touch is just below the pad.

Triggerless Release Aids (Rotational) These were once very popular with target archers and are currently undergoing a revival amongst top shooters. Initially all triggerless release aids were made like this. They are drawn to anchor and as the draw elbow is swung around behind the arrow, the handle is rotated (while the "head" is stuck in place because it is attached to the bowstring) and the release trips itself when rotated "enough." The trick is setting up the release to trigger in the right place (and avoiding that orientation until at full draw and ready to shoot). Since plenty of archers knocked themselves silly by releasing the string when they were pulling hardest, many modern releases of this ilk come with a safety. While the safety is "on" the release will not go off, no matter the orientation. When at full draw, the safety is clicked off and a small additional rotation will cause the shot to be loosed (assuming it was set up right).

This is the release I recommend to most beginning release shooters because they do not have the complication of a trigger and they are way less expensive that the hand-held thumb releases of comparable quality.

Triggerless Release Aids (Straight Pull) These releases don't trigger when rotated, they trigger when they reach a certain draw force. This is typically set about 2# above normal holding weight. You click on a safety that allows you to get through peak weight to your holding weight then click it off at full draw. You just pull a little harder and the thing goes off. These are easily set up with a draw weight scale (the same one you use to measure the holding weight!).

Triggerless Notes These releases have been labeled "back tension releases" when it was thought you need to use back tension to get them to go off. You do not. Any release aid can be shot with or without back tension. No release aid can control the muscles you use in a shot.

Triggerless releases are ideal for trigger-happy youths (as conscious triggering leads to mental issues later) and those on a budget.

The elite archers who are rediscovering the advantages of triggerless releases are generally going for those without safeties in that they are less complicated so less can go wrong. Newer release shooters are better off with a model with a safety for, well, safety's sake. Later they can just stop using the safety and use it without one. The advantages to elite archers are these releases, lacking a trigger, will allow you to monitor when you are moving your body into the full-draw posture and whether than posture is correct (get "out-of-line" and it will go off too soon or too late). And not having a trigger helps them avoid certain forms of "target panic" which can kill a career.

Plus, all release aids need to be first tried using a rope bow and not a real bow. Initial release training needs to be on a rope bow. This is so important that when I first work with a new release archer, I give them a rope bow and ask them to carry it in their quiver at all times. (They never know when they will have the opportunity to try another archer's release.)

Conclusion

We think that when an archer shoots well enough to be able to be fitted for their own equipment, that marks the line between "beginner" and "intermediate" archer. At some point down the line there is a next step. It is when the archer's equipment is exactly fitted to their physical shape, their shooting ability, and their temperament. This requires not only careful fitting but considerable bow-arrow-archer tuning. And an archery axiom is "you can only tune as well as you can shoot," which is why this step can't come earlier.

Additional Learning References

The Bow Fitting by Steve Ruis (AFm, Vol 12, No 2)
Finding the Perfect Fit by Forrest Carter (AFm, Vol 17, No 1)
How Compound Bows Mislead Beginners by Steve Ruis (AFm, Vol 17, No 3)
Bows for Archers with Disabilities by Mitchell Vaughan (AFm, Vol 17, No 2)
On Arrows by Rick McKinney (AFm, Vol 11, No 1)
Arrow Selection by Vittorio Frangilli (AFm, Vol 6, No 1)

When you are coaching never, ever assume things. Take the time to ask your student, so you'll know instead of guessing.

Still More on Coaching Archery

Chapter 31
Coaches Never Assume

I was enjoying a lesson with one of my favorite students just recently and something he said stunned me. He is one of my favorite students because he is over 70, shoots Olympic Recurve, and is still trying to get better . . . and also because I learn a great deal from teaching him.

This was an unusual lesson because he did no shooting, we just talked. We had worked through a few physical issues, then we worked through an equipment issue, and now, he felt, he needed to address the mental game because we still had not got to the core of his inconsistency.

What stunned me was this: he explained in great detail how he mentally talked himself though a shot, through his entire shot sequence, on every shot. You see, I had assumed that he knew that conscious thinking had almost no role to play in executing a shot. My mind was spinning. It immediately jumped to Tom Hank's character in "A League of Their Own" ("Crying? There's no crying in baseball!") and I almost said "Thinking? There's no thinking in archery!" The rest of the lesson consisted of me trying to explain how little conscious thought goes into a normal shot and him not buying much of it.

So, my errors were two: first, I made an assumption about something important and second, I did a lousy job of explaining that something. I have been mulling this over ever since and here is what I have come up with.

And Now for Something Completely Different
We turn to golf? I know, I know, I use a lot of golf analogies and examples but that is only because they are much farther down the road than we are. It wasn't hard to find this quote:

"It's been said a thousand times and it is true;
there's no place for conscious thought in golf." Dave Stockton

If you do not know Dave Stockton, he was a two-time PGA champion, and is unequivocally professional golf's hottest putting and short game instructor. Essentially every golf teacher worth his salt says something similar. This, though, is an overstatement, possibly made for emphasis, but an overstatement nonetheless.

Here's how it goes in golf. Watch any professional golfer on TV execute a shot, it looks outwardly like this: he has a talk with his caddy about the distance of the shot and maybe a few other things, grabs a club and takes a practice swing or two, stands behind the ball looking off into the distance, then steps up to the side of the ball, takes his stance, and swings away. That's what it looks like from the outside. From the inside, this shot began back at the previous one. The golfer has a plan in mind how to approach each hole, if he successfully executed his previous shot, then he knows pretty much what he wants to do next; but how to do that depends on where his ball lies and the quality of that lie and over-hanging tree branches, etc. So, as he is walking up he is checking those things out. When he reaches his ball, he can check out the lie; his caddy is tasked with calculating the distance the next shot has to go and assists in picking a proper landing spot, according to the plan. Once that has been done a club is selected, along with a shot shape (draw, fade, hook, etc.) and a final distance for the shot is settled on (it might be 165 yards to the hole but they may want to land it 20 yards short and let it roll toward the hole, which makes it a 145-yard shot but the slight wind is into his face, so the plan is for a 150-yard shot with the wind knocking it back to 145). Then our golfer takes those few practice swings (thinking about how far he wants the ball to fly with that club), stands behind the ball (visualizing the ball flying through the air with the selected shot shape and landing exactly where desired), steps toward the ball . . . and stops thinking consciously. His execution is done, as they say, by feel; in other words, it is done subconsciously, with no conscious thought. Once the shot is made, a quick evaluation of its outcome and feel are made and then the planning for the next shot is begun.

As in golf, conscious thought in archery is limited to the spaces between shots... and also in practice.

Thinking About Archery

Like our golfer, the conscious mind lays out a flight plan for the unconscious mind to execute, files it, then steps back. We have fewer variables than golfers do: many fewer in target archery, with field archery being closer to golf. And we think our way from shot to shot, but only between shots.

Physical competence resides in your unconscious self. Examples of this are all over the place. Tying your shoes, driving a car, dancing, playing a musical instrument. When we first learn these tasks we have no unconscious competence, so we struggle through them consciously (laboriously, awkwardly, frustratingly) but with practice, the holy grail is achieved: unconscious competence. This is when we perform such acts with ease and grace . . . and success.

Anytime you have achieved some unconscious competence, injecting conscious thought seems to disrupt that execution and you become an awkward beginner again. When this happens, we say we "lost our focus," or some such thing.

When a pro golfer steps into a shot, he passes the borderline between where conscious thought is allowed and where it is forbidden. For archers, this line is, I believe, when the bow is raised. Everything that comes before that point is part of a "pre-shot routine" that helps the archer do everything correctly but the timing of which isn't critical. After the raising of the bow, the timing is critical, and any conscious thoughts are unwelcome.

Practice Thinking The other place conscious thought gets used extensively in golf and archery is during practice. The most effective practices are short in duration and high in intensity. This is because a lot of conscious thinking goes into making instructions for your subconscious mind. If you can remember how you felt after your first driving lesson, that's it. I remember feeling exhausted, drained, and tired, and it seemed like the lesson went on for hours (I think it was 20 minutes). This intensity is necessary to get the subconscious mind's attention and establish the importance of what it is to be learned.

The axiom for archery is: practice consciously and perform subconsciously.

Coaches Never Assume

I had assumed that my student knew this. Coaches never assume: we need to ask, determine and work from reality, not just what we think reality is. Gosh, an Olympic Recurve archer with years of experience and coaching would know this, no? But he did not. It was my job to check in with him about every phase of his game, and since the mental game is hidden from a coach's eyes, this means asking lots of questions. The one that got us started in this particular lesson was "What's going on in your head while making a shot?" I needed to have asked that question much earlier.

But, no harm was done, you say.

I beg to differ. His mental game was masking his physical game under a cloud of inconsistency. With arrow groups being much larger than they needed to be, patterns are much harder to see. This means coaches are less certain about what is going on. Also, when he was in "good form" mentally he shot much better than when he was flagging, so sometimes it looked like we were making progress and other times we were getting worse, but the source of those problems was not what we thought. So the potential (and real) consequences are extra work being done to no avail, the wrong work being done, and lessons being paid for which there wasn't commensurate value.

There was harm done.

Conclusion

When it comes to the mental game, coaches cannot assume anything, as there is no window into an archer's mind. We need to inquire about an archer's mindset, especially asking them "What is going through your head while you are doing X, Y, or Z?"

Additional Learning References

College Archery: The Mental Game, Pt 1 & 2 by Bob Ryder (AFm, Vol 16, No 4 & 5)
Take a Deep Breath by Alison Rhodius (AFm, Vol 12, No 6)
Mental Rehearsal by Troy Bassham (AFm, Vol 12, No 4)
Running a Mental Program by Troy Bassham (AFm, Vol 11, No 5)
Shot Planning by Steve Ruis (AFm, Vol 11, No 3)
Mental Consistency by Lanny Bassham (AFm, Vol 9, No 6)
Should You Pre-load Your Mental Program? by Lanny Bassham (AFm, Vol 8, No 5)
Develop Your Mental Game—How to Begin by Lanny Bassham (AFm, Vol 7, No 5)

Some archers are easier to take than others. And we do get attached to them.

Still More on Coaching Archery

Chapter 32
Managing Emotional Attachments to Athletes

Wow, this is a tough subject. There are a number of dimensions to this issue and although I am not sure how many, I suspect it is large. I know, for instance, that I have a soft spot for older archers still trying to master difficult disciplines, such as Olympic Recurve. I also know I am much less engaged with very young archers who have not yet made a commitment to archery. But this is superficial stuff. Coaches can get heavily invested in the success of their athletes. Yes, archery coaches. I have seen this with parents coaching their own children and I have seen this with coaches who first met their archers in a team tryout/archery class.

Let's explore this.

The Nature of Emotional Attachments
The emotions between coaches and athletes range from positive to negative and mild to strong. An athlete might accept/respect a coach (neutralish), love/admire their coach (positive) or hate/loathe their coach (negative). Occasionally there is mild indifference. Since there is little at stake career-wise or even personally in archery, the intensity of the emotion in the athlete-coach connection is not typically elevated.

Compare archery coaching to gymnastics coaching, for example. In archery coaching, there are few reasons for an athlete and coach to touch or even be in close physical proximity. In gymnastics, coaches may be holding on to an athlete, repositioning their limbs while they are exerting themselves, or hugging them after they complete a routine. The excitement level of a gymnast after mastering or even completing a new movement can be great, whereas archers need to keep a more even emotional keel (it is a "low arousal" sport in sport psychology jargon). So archery does not seem to have waves of emotion that sweep athlete or coach on and that can fuel emotional attachments as they might in other sports. It is important, though, to realize that it is not unnatural to attach one's good feelings to the cause of those good feelings, be it a piece of equipment or a coach.

I do know of coaches and athletes who got married or lived together as such and I do not look on these as being negative. All right, I admit to a bit of prejudice; having been a teacher for over three decades drums a certain propriety into one. Being a teacher or coach is automatically a power position from which to exert influence. Big time coaches in other sports have significantly more power to wield. By "adjusting" playing time, a football or basketball coach can make or break a player who has professional aspirations or even those who are already pros. There are enough athlete-coach squabbles in the news on a continuous basis that support this. Archery coaches, however, unless they are a national team coach don't seem to have that much power. Professional archery is small potatoes compared to other professional sports. Careers in archery don't make one a millionaire. But still, coaches do have a certain standing with athletes, especially when the coach has helped the athlete a great deal, and taking advantage of that standing to build a personal relationship can be problematic.

The Dimensions of Emotional Attachments

There seem to be matters of scale when addressing emotional attachments. Presumably these range from small scale — something like disliking a student enough to not spend time with them or allowing your like for a student to not push them to excel—all the way up to very large scale—something approaching an obsession for a student that freaks everyone out. Obviously the small things do not concern us as much as the big ones.

Inappropriate Attachments What we really want to avoid are inappropriate attachments. Obviously, coaches want to be very (very!) leery of attachments to minors of the opposite sex. Young people can be very attractive in their enthusiasm, work ethic, and sheer joy they take from archery. I certainly appreciate this in young students, but this is a "look but don't touch area" for coaches. If you are spending a lot of time thinking about underage students of the opposite sex and this thinking isn't focused on solving problems they are having with their archery, you are experiencing a warning sign; pay heed.

What If They Are Not Underage? What goes on between consenting adults is an entirely different cup of tea. Here you need only be concerned about the power relationship, and it is rare for archery coaches to be in positions where they can offer much of anything for sexual favors. So, if the attachment is mutual, my opinion is that you are free to explore it. Do realize that if you are a team coach, it will affect team chemistry. If you think you can keep such a relationship hidden, you are wrong.

Professional Detachment What coaches seem to be after in almost every sport is professionalism. Consequently, we encourage archery coaches to act like the professionals they want to be. We even suggest a certain level of dress in our coach training programs. And we strongly urge coaches to charge for their private lessons as this establishes a "fee for service" professional relationship instead of one based upon gratitude even though that may be also involved even when fees are paid.

Part of this professionalism I call "professional detachment," that is, the ability to detach your personal feelings for a student and just consider what you are addressing and not who. I am not saying you need to behave like Mr. Spock; far from it. Coaches who are successful seem to stick closely to their personalities, so they are much the same on the field as off, so to speak. Being yourself is good advice for any archery coach. To be otherwise is to be phony. But your personal "likes" and "dislikes" need to be set aside when you are coaching.

Conclusion

If any of you out there have more experience on this topic, I would love to have you write about it for Archery Focus. Often I do not even have a way to identify someone who could write such an article. We will be very receptive to any such submissions and will pay you for your work.

Additional Learning References

Student Selects Coach / Coach Selects Student by Tom Dorigatti (AFm, Vol 14, No 1)
What Kind of Coach are You? by Tim Scronce (AFm, Vol 8, No 6)

Is there any advice you can give that will guarantee they end up with good form? How about "have fun" as advice?

Still More on Coaching Archery

Chapter 33
On the Nature of Advice

As a coach, you are going to be asked for your opinion, often many times in a session and dozens of times in a day. So, is there a compilation of good advice that you can memorize to have at your call? Is there advice that is always good in all circumstances? This question woke me up and so I am sitting at my computer at 5:20 AM trying to answer it.

Consider an Olympic Recurve student who asks you "Should I look at my clicker while I draw?" This is a "yes or no" kind of question, but I think the only answer is "maybe." There is a lot I would want to know before answering. Coach Kim H.T. of Korea said the answer is generally "yes" for developing archers, but "no" for advanced archers. For advanced-to-elite archers I think this is something that can be trimmed from one's shot sequence as being unnecessary, but even that advice "depends." Obviously having superfluous steps in one's shot sequence does not make sense but the personality of the archer comes into play here. If your student tends to a person who micromanages his shot, I would probably want to discourage watching the clicker as a way to free up his shooting. If, on the other hand, this student was somewhat cavalier with his shot, I might recommend it as a way to get him to be a bit more deliberate.

So, what is needed to be able to give "good" advice to your students? Here is my attempt at the beginning of an answer to this question.

The Foundations of Good Advice

First off, I really don't want to have to define what "good advice" is. I'd rather depend upon your (and my) intuitive understanding of the term. Some advice is good for a time and then turns bad. Some advice is good for one student, bad for another. Some advice is good for a recurve archer, bad for a compound archer. So how the heck are we supposed to sift through all of these effects and come up with consistently good advice?

As Shakespeare said, "Aye, there's the rub."

I do not believe that any advice is absolute. What I mean by this is that there is almost nothing you can say, even to archers of a kind (recurve, longbow, compound) that is always good. (There is a possibility that absolute "bad" advice exists but that is an intellectual discussion we can save for another time. What coach wants to give bad advice?) Claudia, my partner, once said that "Archery is learning to relax and focus under the tension of the draw." This is quite true . . . and it is also possible to be too focused or to be too relaxed to perform well. I often follow up this statement by encouraging my students to relax any muscles not needed to make a shot. One of my older students then shot back that if he were that relaxed, he would fall down. So, I had to qualify the advice that it is important to remain standing while shooting normally, which lead to the mention of bowhunters who shoot from their knees or even while on their backs.

I believe that good advice stems somehow from a depth of understanding. It is not enough to just know that "A causes B;" coaches need to know why A causes B. For example, when a right-handed Olympic Recurve archer's bowstring hits his arm guard, the arrow usually ends up hitting the target face "low and left." This is something that can be memorized. But, if you understand why (the arm guard strike both slows the string down and causes it to rebound away from the archer's arm—the slower string causes a low shot, the string pushed to the right causes a left shot—assuming this happens before the arrow leaves the string) you don't have to memorize that fact and you are in a position to understand similar events. Similarly, Compound–Release archers do not want to use the pads of their thumb or fingers to trigger their release aids (the sensitive finger surface draws too much attention to the trigger when their focus needs to be elsewhere). If you understand what is the source of such dictums, you are in a better position to give advice and to explain "why" to archers who are curious.

You Don't Have to "Do It Right"

I have students who are almost obsessed with "doing it right," as if something magical will happen if they discover exactly how to execute a shot and then do that. We coaches probably brought this upon ourselves as we debate, almost incessantly, the "right ways" to do things. But, as Coach Bernie Pellerite is fond of saying "You don't have to do it right, you just have to do it over."

Elite archers abound who have, shall we say "unusual" form. If you saw the gold medal winning shot in the 2012 (London) Olympics Men's Team competition, you will immediately realize that Michele Frangilli has. . . , well, . . . idiosyncratic form. Nobody shoots anywhere near to the way Michele does. As a coach, would I recommend that he "fix" any of his "form flaws?" Absolutely not! Here is why. If an archer adopts a "personal style," one that is not optimal for him/her, there is a cost to doing so. Typically it is a training cost. One will need to train harder or longer to make that particular form or execution element consistent. If one has paid that price, why would one pay even more changing to another way to shoot that isn't guaranteed to be better?

This is why, as coaches, we stress shooting close to "textbook style" to beginning and intermediate archers. This recommendation is close to what should be "optimal form" for most people, so why would you recommend anything else if it would only make learning more difficult?

This is then a key question: when should you recommend something that isn't "textbook?" The clear answer is: when "textbook" doesn't work. I managed to talk the Coaches Development Committee of USA Archery into including a segment in its Level 4 Coach training on "Adapting Standard Form." (This never got realized because the project that would have developed the training materials got cancelled before it was written.) Obviously we adapt standard form for disabled archers, often radically so, but in reality "textbook form" is adapted to every archer. Nobody shoots perfect textbook form.

I was assigned the task to develop the training segment and the best I could come up with was to have a roundtable discussion about cases in which archers were urged to do something different to overcome a limitation to standard form. I had nothing else because nobody to my knowledge has written about this. (I have subsequently, but nobody else has.) My hope was to learn enough from the roundtable discussions to cobble some useful materials together.

Hurdles to Standard Form

We start training archers with descriptions of standard form. What they end up with is slightly different. Typically this is a trial-and-test situation where the archer tries and adapts, tries and adapts, until he finds something that works. Sometimes coaches are asked to advise.

I have a student who has very well-developed shoulders (a former gymnast). You may have noticed that elite archers tend to be a bit on the skinny side. This is because archers use leverage instead of muscle when shooting. Large shoulder muscles can inhibit the movement of the shoulder blades (scapulae) into the positions that allow the back muscles to "hold" the drawn bow. Years of archery do not create large shoulder muscles, like male gymnasts get from years of gyming?, gymnasting?

This very student was having trouble with high fliers, often wildly high fliers. The problem stemmed from his interpretation of a textbook admonition that the draw elbow must move in an arc (about 20°-30° down and around) continuously through the shot once the draw is complete. Unfortunately his back muscles blocked this movement just short of him being "in line" but he kept the elbow moving anyway as he could feel it move. Unfortunately, when his shoulders blocked his scapulae from moving in toward his spine, the draw elbow kept moving all right, but straight down. This changed the angle of his fingers on the string, causing "high fliers." In the end, we had to trade off the danger of plucks from a draw elbow not quite in line as being smaller than the dropping draw elbow that caused disastrous high fliers (even off of the target at 30 m).

An archer's flexibility, size, strength, coordination, muscle masses, natural tempo (I don't know the source of this) and, I suspect, a large number of other factors affect his ability to perform. A great many physical limitations can be overcome with ingenuity and perseverance (for evidence just look to the nearest disabled archer). To be a great archer there is one ability that is absolutely necessary: the ability to not get bored easily.

Helping with working around limitations, both physical and mental, is an important function of coaches and we need to start taking better notes collectively so we can learn to do this better.

Conclusion

I am going to go out on a limb here to say that all, every little bit, of archery form and execution involves multiple tradeoffs. Because of this, archers can and do shoot extremely well while violating the precepts of "good form." Each archer's form, while similar to every other archer of the same equipment style, is unique to them in the small bits. Helping our students to find "their shot," and then helping them to learn to "own it" requires us to be focused on a great many things that archers do not need to know. We need to know a lot more of the "whys" of archery form and execution so we can help our students with advice on the "whats" and "hows."

So, every chance you get to learn something of the "whys" of archery is a chance for you to become a better coach.

Additional Learning References

Form Flaws Corrected by Larry Wise (AFm, Vol 17, No 6)
Correcting Poor Shooting Form by Larry Wise (AFm, Vol 16, No 1)
The Lines of Archery by Steve Ruis (AFm, Vol 16, No 1)
Where Form Flaws Come From by Steve Ruis (AFm, Vol 11, No 3)
B.E.S.T. or Better? by Steve Ruis (AFm, Vol 10, No 5)
Shooting Form Analysis by Van Webster (AFm, Vol 9, No 6)
Teaching Form by Steve Ruis (AFm, Vol 9, No 5)

Are your instructions clear or are you speaking in code . . . archery code.

Still More on Coaching Archery

Chapter 34
Watch Your Language!

As beginning coaches we are admonished to "keep it positive!" to "never describe what they are doing wrong" and to "always describe how to do it right." All of this is good advice but it isn't the whole story, by far, when it comes to coaches watching their language.

Obviously we want to avoid statements like "Don't grab the bow." For one it sounds like a criticism and most of us, especially if your archer is young, he probably has enough of that already. The other is it doesn't tell one what to do instead.

But what about statements like: "stand up tall?" This is a recipe for doing it right, no? This phrase is often used to correct beginners who are hunched over their shots, often because they are trying to sight down their arrow in the mistaken belief that doing so will help them hit the target. What I have observed, though, is that young archers, especially, mistake what is wanted, and actually stand too tall. They arch their backs, their heads tilt back. They over correct from one mistake into another. Too often I have seen coaches give this exact instruction and then move on to another student without refining their directive to get the young athlete into the correct position.

This is falling into a coach's trap, the *Trap of Magic Words*.

The Magic Words Trap

Most coaches started as archers who learned a lot of archer's jargon. Part of joining any group is learning the special language of the group, the understanding of which is necessary to feel part of the group. So, you learn what "plucking" means and you learn what "grabbing your bow means" and you learn what "punching your release" means, and "peeking," "creeping," and "collapsing."

I remember the first time my "coach" (*aka* friend and mentor) told me I was "punching" shots. I had been a boxer since middle school and I was absolutely certain that I had at no time either punched anything archery-related or even tried to punch anything archery-related. I was completely perplexed and, even though I was an adult, strangely reluctant to ask for a clarification.

We in archery are not unique in this. I overheard a golf lesson that used the phrases "getting to your front side," "stuck at the top," and "clear your hips." Know what they mean? Neither do I.

These archery words do communicate a great deal . . . to archers who are masters of archery jargon, but for beginners, eh, not so much. The Trap of the Magic Words for coaches is thinking that they mean something to the uninitiated. To tell a beginner, "you dropped your bow," when they are standing there, bow in hand knowing full well they hadn't dropped it; they can only end up wondering what the heck you are talking about. Of course, they think you mean "dropped your bow onto the ground." "You dropped your bow" is a contraction of "you dropped your bow arm" which is a contraction of "you dropped your bow arm during the shot." These are all jargon for not holding one's bow arm still during a shot.

We are all susceptible to this trap, because we get tired of explaining what "grabbing the bow" means or what "creeping" means or what "back tension" means. We want these shortcuts to save us from long explanations.

All I can say is you know the job was tough when you took it. Archery is a repetition sport. Coaching archery is a repetition job, too.

Conclusion

Basically, employing the same language used to describe subtleties for advanced archers with the uninitiated is a recipe for mistakes. Possible the best solution is simply to adhere to the requirements of good communication. When you say something, you need to look to see if what you said was heard and also understood. It doesn't hurt to "check in" with your archers to see if they understood, if for no other reason than if they did not, you just wasted your effort and you will have to do it over shortly anyway.

Monitor yourself to see if you use "archery jargon" with people who don't know the terms. As with shooting arrows, it is easier if you can relegate to the realm of habit those things that need to be repeated often. So, if you have bad habits, turn them into good habits and you will save both time and energy.

Additional Learnng References
Finding Coaching Wisdom by Steve Ruis (AFm, Vol 15, No 4)
The Elements of Good Practice by AER (AFm, Vol 15, No 3)
Situational Coaching by Tom Barker & Steven Swade (AFm, Vol 13, No 5)
How to Teach Archery by Steve Ruis (AFm, Vol 12, No 5)
Adapting Archery for People Who Have Disabilities by Randi Smith (AFm, Vol 11, No 5)
Teaching or Coaching by Tim Scronce (AFm, Vol 10, No 3)
What Kind of Coach are You? by Tim Scronce (AFm, Vol 8, No 6)

Let's chop up an archer. . . ?

Still More on Coaching Archery

Chapter 35
Toward a Common Terminology

One of the problems we have as coaches is confusion over the terms we use. Recurve archers use the terms "front half" and "back half" but compounders don't. We are all confused when we use terms like "to the rear of the archer" or "in back of the archer" as we think they mean both standing on the shooting line so you can see the archer's back and standing away from the archer in line with the target so you can see the archer's draw elbow.

We also can't use simple terms like "elbow" or "left elbow" because there are two elbows and they are used for different purposes, which are reversed between left- and right-handed archers.

It would be nice to have terms that we can all use no matter the style or handedness and with little or no confusion about their meanings. Here's my attempt at the beginnings of such.

Let's Chop Up a Bow

We already have decent agreements and terms in bow terminology and I don't want to rename the parts of bows, but there are some supporting principles that help us and we should make them more clear. For example: all directions are from the viewpoint of the archer. This is why archers refer to the outside edge of the bow as the back of the bow and outsiders tend to refer to it as the front of the bow. Making sure everyone understands this basic agreement will help get everybody clear and concise.

The one term I think we need to add to our lexicon is string plane. Target bows are shot with a vertical string plane (whereas crossbows are shot with a roughly horizontal string plane). A condition for accuracy then is for the target center and the arrow to be in the same vertical plane. This is, coincidentally, the plane in which the force of gravity operates on the arrow. If the arrow is in a plane other than the vertical plane going through target center, it is being aimed "off" and you are hoping something, like wind, affects the arrow's flight to push it into that plane and into the target center. The closer the string stays to that plane, the more likely it is that we will have minimal windage error. Yes, one can "cant" a bow and it performs equally well but how consistently can you cant your bow? Also, canting a bow using a bow sight results in left-right mistakes based upon moving the aperture out of the vertical plane (changing the vertical and horizontal relationship of aperture to arrow). Up and down we can all find fairly well as we have built-in physiological clues (balance, etc.)

and there are environmental clues (edges of buildings, trunks of straight trees, etc.). So finding straight up and down is easier and therefore more consistent. The string plane supplies a term useful in describing both the orientation and function of a target bow.

Let's Chop Up an Archer

This could be more complicated, but I adhere to the KISS principle, so won't go too far. Some terms will likely stick around. For example, compound archers may want to keep the term "release hand" (I can't see that term disappearing soon), but it obviously does not apply to recurve bow, longbow, or crossbow archers. So, here are some suggestions on the parts of an archer and orientations of the same.

Since "front/back" or "in front/behind" are so confusing, how about this: target archers hold a bow in one hand and manipulate/pull the string with the other, so let's call the entire side of the archer that is holding on to the bow the bow side and the entire side of the archer that is connecting with the string (with a tab or release or whatever) the string side. These terms work no matter what style of bow you use, save crossbows. So the bow side consists of: a bow hand, a bow wrist, a bow arm (with a bow elbow), and a bow shoulder. If you want to talk about the knee, foot, or hip on that same side, you can use the terms: bow knee, bow foot, or bow hip if you want. Some already use terms like "bow-side foot" or bow-side hip." The new terms are just a bit shorter. On the string side of the archer are: a string hand, a string wrist, a string arm (with a string elbow), and a string shoulder. If you want to talk about the knee, foot, or hip on that same side, you can use the terms: string knee, string foot, or string hip if you want. If compound folks want to use release hand instead of string hand, I don't think that will confuse anybody.

Let's Chop Up The Space Around an Archer

Again, there is so much confusion around "front/back" or "in front/behind" when it comes to viewpoints from which to observe an archer, it is no wonder that the terms "Coaching Position #1, #2, #3, and #4" were invented. But then the definitions of those positions changed (one of the four used to involve a quartering view of the archer; that was replaced by a view looking over the string elbow at full draw) and, well, they aren't particularly descriptive terms, so if your memory is at all faulty, instant confusion ensues.

Let's keep faith with the principle that "all directions are from the viewpoint of the archer" and use front and back/rear to mean what they mean to the archer. If you are in front of the archer, you are standing on the shooting line facing the archer's chest. If you are in back of the archer, you are standing on the shooting line facing the archer's back. (Now, isn't that simple?)

It is a little harder for the other two points on the archer's compass, and I do want the terms to be short, if possible, so I picked the position of the target as our indicator. I could have recommended "target side" but that leaves us with what "not the target side" for the opposite! So, I chose toward and away. These are contractions of "toward the target" and "away from the target" but just the words toward and away carry the question with them "toward what?" and "away from what" – and what is the biggest focal point on an archery range? The target. So, these are short, snappy, and do the trick. If I told you to stand in front of an archer and away, I think most people would find the right spot fairly easily. Terms like this will still need to be taught; an outsider might think that "in front of an archer and away" meant they would stand between the archer and the target but at a greater distance, but that's the cost of using short words for such terms.

Another option would be to use a horizontal clock face: Coach's 3 o'clock would be the same as front, Coach's 6 o'clock would be the same as away, and Coach's 9 o'clock would be the same as back. This is a more precise system as we could refer to a coaching position at 4:30, half way between 3 and 6, for example. We could shorten these to "Coach's 6" or even "6 o'clock" as in "I was observing the archer at 6 o'clock, close in and I noticed…"

Conclusion

What do you think? Got better ideas? With terms, they either live or die through use. If you like these terms, use them. If you don't, do not. 'S'all you gotta do.

It would be nice, though, if we all used the same terms.

Additional Learning References

The Lines of Archery by Steve Ruis (AFm, Vol 16, No 1)
Golf Envy, Part Deux by Steve Ruis (AFm, Vol 14, No 4)
Word Search for the Archery Linguist (A Puzzle) by Tom Dorigatti (AFm, Vol 9, No 3)
Why Does Canting Work? by Aaron Stone (AFm, Vol 7, No 4)

You see these lines, don't you?

Still More on Coaching Archery

Chapter 36
What to Look For (At?)

For Beginning-to-Intermediate Coaches

Most coaches start out teaching youths in a "class setting," that is as part of a JOAD or 4-H shooting program, for example. (I started in our club's 4-H program. Yes, you can blame them.) If you take to coaching there comes a time in which you make the transition between teaching a group and teaching individuals. So, an archer approaches you for "a lesson" and you agree to meet with them. There is a great deal to talk about during the lesson, but I like to weave much of that in as the prospective student is setting up their bow, warming up, and shooting some arrows. The topic of this chapter is: while they are shooting, what do you look for (at)?

I am recommending a somewhat systematic approach, even though advanced coaches don't necessarily do this. The reason some more advanced coaches don't necessarily follow a step-by-step approach is that once your eye is trained, the things that aren't right simply jump out and announce themselves. I assume you have, sometime in your life, seen a Chess Master play many games simultaneously. The master walks from board to board, pausing only for a second or two at most, makes a move and moves to the next board. (I have participated in several of these master class exhibitions, but the game was Go.) Did you wonder how that person could keep all of those games in memory? The answer is that he/she didn't. One glance at the board was all that was needed to see what was going on. There are masters who can do this blindfolded and they are certainly doing it from memory, but if they can see the board, why bother memorizing it when everything important just jumps out.

I remember when this first happened to me. I was walking down the line (in the spectator area) of an NAA Outdoor Championship line and pop, pop, pop . . . things in each archer's form stood out. These things were not necessarily wrong, they were just . . . I think the right word is incongruous, that is, incompatible, inconsistent, or in Sesame Street terms, "one of these things is not like the others."

Until you have trained your eye, this is not an option, so what should you do to train your coaching eye?

General Approach

Some Preliminaries I like to watch an archer set up to shoot. You will get an impression of how meticulous they are about their equipment. Is their equipment shiny and new? older and well-used? mis-matched or ill-suited to the archer? You can also see how comfortable they are in using it. A bow that has been shot a great deal can be likened to a well-broken-in baseball glove; it becomes an extension of your body. Much of this can be seen simply by watching the archer prepare to shoot. Obviously you can observe this while you are talking; I am not recommending you hover over the archer like a vulture.

I also want to see how they approach their first shots. Do they step up to the line and empty their quiver? Do they seem to have a routine? Do they warm up blank bale or do they use a target?

A Structured Approach I have said often enough that an archer's shot sequence forms a structure for coaching. It serves so here, essentially because the archer is displaying their shot sequence in front of your eyes. I usually ask students if they know the term "shot sequence" as many do not. If they do not, it is unlikely that they have addressed it consciously.

Stance Since the stance is the first step in taking a shot, so I pay quite a bit of attention to it. Obvious things like "open, closed, or square" are noted (you take notes, no?) but also important things like "is the stance consistent?" Does the archer move his/her feet unnecessarily (often when loading another arrow or reaching for an arrow in a ground quiver)?

Nocking an Arrow This may be a trivial thing but, as all things in archery, it is absolutely important when you are doing it. In addition to whether it was done well, was it done consistently? Are they loading their bow vertically, thus not invading the space of an archer only a couple of feet away? Are the arrow's nocks all set the same (to give the same fletch clearance possibilities for each shot)?

Setting the Hands How meticulously is this done? Is it consistent? Most archers have bowhand problems so this is an area I focus on a great deal. The bowhand is the only area of contact with the bow as the arrow is leaving. It absolutely must be "relaxed." Many archers have a "pistol grip" and/or "death grip" that must be fixed early on to achieve consistent accuracy.

Raising the Bow Does the bow come up and stop . . . or does it come up and then come down (a little or a lot)? Raising the bow above where it is needed and then lowering it wastes energy and creates an inconsistent bow arm/shoulder. The bow should come up to where it is needed and then drawn. Is this done consistently? If there is a predraw included, is it consistent?

Drawing the String Is the draw smooth and strong? It is my observation that many females draw too slowly and many males draw too quickly (why I do not know). Neither is desirable. Drawing too slowly wastes energy and reduces the time available at full draw that is calm and relaxed. Drawing too quickly sets up extraneous motions that take time to dampen as well as move the archer's aperture off location, necessitating it being moved back.

Finding the Anchor Is the anchor tight and firm? Is the archer relaxed? Is the anchor position consistent? This is another area which requires a great deal of focus (along with the bowhand). Unnecessary tension in the draw hand or forearm leads to poor releases and is very common so I pay special attention to this.

Aiming Not much to look for here, but if there is considerable movement of the bow after anchor, work needs to be done on the "raise" segment to get the bow into position. One does not want to waste time at full draw moving the bow around.

Release Obvious things to look for are plucking (fingers) and punching (release)...

more on those below. I like to watch the string (aka rear or draw) elbow tip at release. Is it moving in a slightly downward, mostly backward arc? Is it moving at all (if not, a static or dead release is involved)? If it is moving straight downward, expect a lot of high fliers. If it is moving back along the path it took, the archer is creeping or collapsing.

Followthrough Critical aspects of an uninvolved bow hand and a strong bow arm, so the things to look for are the bow jumping out straight from the hand and the bow arm staying up. Watch the tip of the stabilizer (if a long rod is used). It should jump forward an inch or so before moving off in what I like to call the bow's bow (as in when actors "take a bow"). Sighting along any part of the bow arm with some part of the background will allow you to see if the bow arm stays up during this phase.

Some Specific Things to Look At (Fingers Shooters)

Additional information can be gleaned from examining the accessories "fingers" shooters use. Here are some examples.

Tabs Take a look at your archer's finger tab. There should be a single indentation in the tab's top surface, made by the pressure of the bowstring. If that indentation is much wider than the bowstring, the setting of the finger hook varies in depth, e.g. sometimes a deep hook, sometimes a not-so-deep hook. If that indentation is hourglass shaped, then the archer's string hand is varying in the angle it makes with the bowstring. Tabs that are very worn need to be replaced or have new "leathers" fitted, then broken in.

Armguards I remember when I first met Rick McKinney. He decided to join our winter indoor league. One of the first things I noticed was his armguard. There was a little scuffed patch on his armguard, maybe a quarter of an inch in length, where his bowstring hit it. The fact that the scuffed patch was so small was a testament to his consistency (he had one of the best bow arms in American archery history).

Some Specific Things to Look At (Release Shooters)

Release shooters require some special attention.

Trigger Finger Positions No matter whether they are using a handheld release (preferred by most target archers) or a wristrap release, there are some common aspects that need to be observed. If the release aid has a trigger, the actuating digit (finger, thumb, pinkie) must be off the trigger until after anchor position is obtained. Wristrap release shooters usually tuck their "trigger finger" behind the trigger while drawing and anchoring, then swing it around.

Punching the Trigger Consciously setting the release off is not desired. This is often referred to as "punching" the trigger. What is desired is for the trigger to be slowly squeezed. If you see a finger or thumb jump back in the direction of the trigger when the shot occurs, they are probably punching. You should see no movement of that digit. One mechanical problem may compound this problem and that is trigger pressure. Some releases do not have adjustab;e trigger pressures and some that do only have very light setting available. The trigger pressure (measured in ounces of force) should be fairly high, making it easy to get on the trigger without the worry of setting the thing off.

Release Aid Fit and Setup Release aids have to fit your archer's hand, wrist, and personality. If you have a fidgety archer, maybe a triggerless release is better. If calm and methodical, almost any kind of release aid might work. If the wriststrap is loose on the wrist, draw length will vary. If the trigger is not positioned so that it avoids contact with the thumb pad or finger pad used on it, it needs adjusting (finger and thumb tips are too sensitive to provide a "surprise release").

Behind It All
In lessons just the day before writing this I had two teenaged young ladies who, since their last lesson, had acquired a large flourish with their release hands after their strings were loosed. Since these two participate in a youth archery program, I am not the only one giving instruction (plus we always have to deal with advice "volunteered" by other archers). We clearly needed to deal with the extraneous motions. Any motion not associated with the shot makes it more difficult to keep track of the motions that are.

It is vitally important that coaches distinguish between "things that are done" and "things that happen" during shots. A finger shooter's hand will run back along their face as part of their followthrough if . . . if they are using the correct muscles to draw the bow and release the string. So if their release hand is "dead" or not moving correctly, should you tell them what their release hand is supposed to do? Please do not, certainly not at the beginning. Work at getting them to draw the bow by rotating their string (aka rear or draw) shoulder back and around. If the muscles responsible for that are still operating when the string fingers relax, the hand will involuntarily move back along the face until the fingers are approximately under the archer's ear.

If you mention "what their hand should do" they will make their hand do it, as my two young students did, and you will not only have not made any progress; instead, you will have helped them to create a habit that has no value and will have to be trained out.

Be sure you know what is "done" and what "happens as a result" in a shot. Teach "what is done" and allow "what happens" to happen, then show your students that those happenings are signs of what was done being done right, *e.g.* "if you are properly using your back muscles, your string hand will slide back along your face, ending up with your fingers under your ear."

Conclusion
Whatever you adopt as a routine to evaluate the form and execution of your students, new or otherwise, take notes and make it part of your education as a coach to pay attention to how you work. This includes working with students with widely different personalities and different archery styles. The more you learn about archery and yourself, the better you become as a coach.

Additional Learning References
Teaching Kids to Use Release Aids by Larry Wise (AFm, Vol 16, No 3)
The Lines of Archery by Steve Ruis (AFm, Vol 16, No 1)
Correcting Poor Shooting Form by Larry Wise (AFm, Vol 16, No 1)
So You Want to Emulate a Pro? by Tom Dorigatti (AFm, Vol 14, No 4)
The Whole and Its Parts by Steve Ruis (AFm, Vol 13, No 3)
Adapting Archery for People Who Have Disabilities, Pt 2 by Randi Smith (AFm, Vol 11, No 5)
Shooting Form Analysis by Van Webster (AFm, Vol 9, No 6)

Al Henderson was one of the finest archery coaches ever born in this country. He coached Olympic Champions on down to little kids. He was inducted into the Archery Hall of Fame in 1982 . . . as a coach. As an archer, he was good, but not great.

Chapter 37
Why Great Archers Don't Necessarily Make Great Coaches

I know this is going to tick off quite a few people, so I apologize for any offense you may take in advance, but hear me out. It is the case in most sports that the great performers don't necessarily make good coaches. Think of Ted Williams in baseball, Bill Russell in basketball, or Wayne Gretsky in hockey. None of these guys will be remembered as great coaches. If you make lists of great coaches you will find that many of them were very, very good as players, but very few were great. The only one I can think of is John Wooden, who is in the Basketball National Hall of Fame as both a player and as a coach.

Is this also true for archery? I think it is. When I think of great coaches who also were great archers about the only name that comes to mind is Terry Wunderle. Larry Wise was a very good archer but was not dominant. Al Henderson? Nope. Lloyd Brown? Nope. KiSik Lee? He had flashes of brilliance. Larry Sullivan? Nope. Bernie Pellerite? Nope. George Chapman was a very, very good archer, but again, not dominant. If you start with a list of the very best archers, you will likewise find very few dominant coaches on that list.

Why?

Some of the reasons are those shared with other sports. Some say that great athletes are so used to performing at a high level that they cannot understand why somebody with great talent can't do likewise, or that it is a failing of the great athlete to appreciate the struggles of the less prominent. Others point out that many superstars isolate themselves because they feel they have few peers, which makes it hard for them to relate to merely mortal performers.

I think archery is probably similar. But, the viewpoints of archers and archery coaches are radically different. The archer's viewpoint is from the inside out. The coach's viewpoint is from the outside in. The archer can't see what the coach can see (this is less so now due to video recording capabilities) and the coach can't feel what the archer feels. So, a lot of communication is need for coach and archer to make things work.

In addition, to be a top performer, meaning a consistent winner, you don't need to learn five different ways to do any one thing well, but to be a coach, you may have to be able to suggest a number of different ways to do the same thing because not all archers are equally capable. Nor are all archers the same in how they learn; what appeals to one athlete may not appeal to another. I think a major factor is that archers who are "good" but not "great" need to find an edge (or more likely a bunch of edges) to advance themselves. Their ability level alone doesn't cut it. So, they are always on the prowl for new knowledge, new equipment, new procedures. Great archers can avoid such distractions. They need to work on their shot, not everyone's shots. They need to learn to shoot the bow their sponsor gave them, not survey the whole bow market to find the bows that work best for them.

Less accomplished but ambitious archers are constantly looking for ways to break through to higher levels, so they are always looking for ways to maximize their ability. This translates well to coaching as our students are looking for help in boosting their own abilities. Coaches with this background have more experience to draw from as well a wide base of empathy to connect with our students.

So, If I Can Get a Lesson from a Top Archer, Should I?

I would go for it. But I would prepare like crazy for that lesson. You may also need to explore whether you can benefit from the lesson. How many things might you get to ask about? You may want to write out all of your questions and have that list handy. I would list all of the strengths and weaknesses I see in my shot so I can compare that with what the coach sees. The coach may want to focus in on the one part of my shot that he/she thinks they can help me with, so I want to have those things in mind.

As a general rule, I am more of a coach than I am an archer at my age, but I look to get lessons from any top coach I connect with. Maybe they can help my shooting but I also get to see them work as a coach as well, so I get a double lesson: one on shooting and one on coaching and that makes the lesson fee a real bargain.

Additional Learning References

Adapting Standard Form by Steve Ruis (AFm, Vol 16, No 6)
The Lines of Archery by Steve Ruis (AFm, Vol 16, No 1)
Student Selects Coach/Coach Selects Student by Tom Dorigatti (AFm, Vol 14, No 1)
Archery Coaches—Born or Made? by Randi Smith (AFm, Vol 13, No 2)

What do golf coaches know that we do not? Apparently a lot.

Still More on Coaching Archery

Chapter 38
What the Coach Knows and
the Athlete Needs

I often say to those I coach that coaches have an "outside in" viewpoint while archers have an "inside out" viewpoint and it takes both viewpoints to make significant progress. When I train coaches I harp on this point. This is the mistake that people who think that "good archers should be good coaches" make. Coaches need to be trained as to what to look for and what and how to communicate what they see. A key aspect of this difference between coach and athlete is the difference between what the coach needs to know and what the athlete needs to know.

An Athlete Needs . . .

Athletes need feedback. They can't see what they look like in any particular body position and coaches often have to provide that feedback. I watched a video of Golf Coach Hank Haney working with a fairly accomplished amateur golfer. (There are dozens of these videos available from golf coaches; wouldn't it be nice if world-class archery coaches posted videos of them working with accomplished students!) Coach Haney explained what he saw in this golfer's swing and then he described a corrective. He actually physically placed the golfer in the body position he was looking for at the "top" of the swing. Then he asked the golfer to take a "practice swing" doing as he requested. The guy was not even close. As the lesson progressed, Coach Haney repositioned the student's arms and hands at the top of the swing and asked the guy to somehow get there (multiple times—patience is a required attribute of coaches). After dozens of practice swings and hit balls, the guy was halfway between his old swing and what Coach Haney was asking him to do. Which also turned out to be exactly where Mr. Haney wanted him. His instructions were deliberately overstated because he knew that the "old form" would pull the golfer back toward it, so he recommended a gross exaggeration so that when the golfer felt "that," he was actually in the right position and not the recommended one. (I call this the Goldilocks' Principle of Coaching.)

Throughout this lesson, Coach Haney was giving feedback to the golfer, telling him how his swing looked so he could match it to how it felt to him. This is what athletes need: feedback (on top of good instruction and encouragement).

Golf has gone Gonzo in this direction. They have made radar monitors that give instantaneous feedback on golf shots, including how fast the ball left the club and what angle the club was traveling and how "square" the club was to the direction desired. They even make little boxes that clip onto your club shaft which tell you how fast the club head was moving during a swing. They have similar devices for putting as well. They have video cameras on a stick that you can thrust into the turf to take videos of your swing. (Yes, I have golf envy.)

Scientific studies have shown that immediate feedback is the most important factor in programming body movement. Experiments have shown that movements can be trained through feedback even without the subject being aware of what needed to be done. The subjects were just told to maximize the quality of the feedback. In one experiment, back in the 70s, subjects were able to change their heart rates based on feedback without being told they were to do anything! (The feedback was a flashing light and the subjects were put in a boring room. The wavering in the rate of flashing caused the bored minds of the subjects to attempt to see if the could affect the rate of flash. In one case, the subjects actually raised their blood pressure while reducing their heart rate as that was what would make the light flash faster.)

Some athletes, though, are curious and want to know what is behind certain recommendations (adults more so than kids, in my experience). Is there any advantage to them knowing the details? There does not seem to be, other than the coach establishing that he does know what he is talking about, as nothing in the background information actually helps the athlete to perform. In essence the athlete is saying "tell me what to *do*."

What the Coach Knows

Recently a young coach I am mentoring asked me a question regarding something that he had heard that contradicted something I had taught him. The bottom line was I encouraged him to keep asking questions because people say all kinds of things, whether or not they have strong evidence for their opinions. People also repeat things told to them by others. There is a lot of BS floating around. I urged this young man to judge everything for himself, to think through things he was being told, including the things that I was telling him. Now, I know that my scientific training is showing through here. In science, authority is not a source of truth. "Because so and so said so," will not win you any scientific arguments. And I think archery coaches would be a lot better off if we had the same attitude.

The caveat to this approach is coaches need to know enough to evaluate various "claims" made by archers and other coaches. Coaches need to learn a little biomechanics, a little anatomy, a little physics, a little engineering, a little about nutrition, a little about physical training and, most of all, know when they have exhausted their own knowledge. (This is one of the things I am working on. I often think I know more than I do, so I have to be cautious.) When you have exhausted your knowledge, you need to develop sources you can ask for help. I have been blessed with the editorship of Archery Focus magazine, so I have come into contact with a great many experts I can beg help from. Obviously most archery coaches don't have such resources but they need to develop some ways to acquire what they do not already know. (This is why I have been promoting the creation of a professional archery coaches association, which could compile such resources and make them available to the rank and file.)

So it is that coaches need to know "why" as well as "what." And they need to know that athletes don't really need the "why" so much.

Conclusion

Unlike the golf market, the market for "archery feedback gizmos" is miniscule. Huge numbers of golf training aids are sold every year. I wish I had a piece of the action on the GPS distance finders golfers now use. These handheld devices (often cell phone apps) tell you how far you are from the pin, the front of the green, various hazards, etc. on thousands of golf courses. These things are selling like hotcakes and they aren't cheap. But, unlike golf, our arrows should leave our bows at the same speed each and every time, so even if you do have a chronograph, it won't help you train much. A shooting machine might help you get all of your arrows matched but they won't completely tune them if you are using a finger release. Not a lot of these devices are sold as a consequence. Coaches still tend to be the primary source of feedback.

Maybe in Korea archers always have a coach present when they are shooting, but that doesn't happen here in the U.S. Coaches meet with their archers and send them off to practice on their own. But no coach, no feedback. So, some things can be done to fill in this void. One possibility is to have a shooting partner who can step into the role of "Feedback Giver" for things that need an "outside-in" viewpoint. In the absence of another person, the old tried-and-true method is for the archer to use mirrors to examine their body positions. Video cameras can be used to make records (with and without the use of mirrors) that can be sent to the coach for feedback (delayed feedback) and can also be reviewed right after being recorded by the archer (immediate feedback). This practice requires that the archer fill both viewpoints (outside-in and inside-out) but it is better than nothing.

I met a guy who took a multi-camera home security system and set the cameras up to view himself shooting from four sides and above, all of which can be replayed instantly on a laptop computer screen. I asked the guy to write about how he built it but he didn't end up doing that. If anyone has built such a rig, I am very interested in providing that information to others and will pay you for an article for *Archery Focus*. Email me at steve@archeryfocus.com.

Additional Learning References

Coach's Eye by Bob Ryder (AFm, Vol 17, No 5)
The Lines of Archery by Steve Ruis (AFm, Vol 16, No 1)
Coaching with a Camera by A Ron Carmichael (AFm, Vol 13, No 2)
Video as a Training Tool by Mark Lonsdale (AFm, Vol 6, No 1)

General Commentary

What ever you do, don't let down as you'll run out of time!
(Photo Courtesy of Kathy Miller)

Still More on Coaching Archery

Chapter 39
Alternate Shot Competition
Letdown Strategies and Alternatives

Watching the archery competitions at the London Olympics on my computer was a delight. In the past we got very little live television coverage and had to order a DVD to view highlights. Now we got to see significant portions of the competitions. This was most welcome.

One of the things that stood out, in my mind, was the number of poor shots made following quite good shots in the alternate shot format. A ten would be followed by a six. At first I thought it was due to the pressure, but I had seen some of those archers perform better under similar pressures. I then realized the issue was the clock.

In the 2008 FITA Rules, archers were given 30 seconds to make a shot. As of 2010, they were only given 20 seconds. With a twenty-second clock, if one gets too deep into a shot before realizing that a letdown is in order, then there is insufficient time to execute the letdown and get off the next shot. What I was seeing was archers desperately trying to get off a flawed shot.

This is not good archery.

But my opinion doesn't count for much. I did offer a solution and that was to use a chess clock setup. Both archers begin with one minute on their clocks (3 shots x 20 seconds per shot = 60 seconds). When the match begins, the first archer's clock starts ticking. When they finish their shot, they hit a nearby button that stops their clock and starts their opponents. If they only need 15 seconds to get off each of their first two shots, they would have 30 seconds for the third. In effect, they could execute one letdown on one of their three shots and still score all three arrows optimally.

Technical fixes aside, the question arises: how are we going to train archers to deal with this situation? A number of alternatives occur to me.

Gutting It Out at Full Draw What the archers were doing in London was just this. Had they trained to do so? Was there a mental program to run in such an occasion? I am not a fan of this approach as an archer can get locked up physically from having been still too long. But it might appeal to some, so it should be considered as an option. Another reason I don't like it is one would end up practicing shooting incorrectly. Practice of this approach will be needed and I believe a mental program as well.

One practice motif would be standing with your archer on the shooting line, with a stopwatch, and making them wait 5-10 seconds at full draw before finishing. I wouldn't do this continuously but arrange a signal for maybe one shot out of three or so, maybe the word "wait" followed by the word "finish" after the waiting period. I would be looking for a deliberate finish, not a rushed one because the athlete was running out of gas at full draw. Any number of variations exist.

When practicing alone, the archer can give themselves a count of 1-10 to count off at full draw before finishing a shot. The bulk of these should be short, with only occasional longer ones.

These sessions need to be short so as to not distort normal form. The ideal, of course, is the archer always shoots in rhythm.

Learning to Shoot Faster This approach has more merit than the one above, in my opinion. There are benefits to shooting faster. The Koreans have data showing that shooting more quickly produces more consistency. This, of course, can only be "up to a point." Trying to get three quality shots off in 10 seconds is probably impossible. But here our goal would be to get two shots off comfortably within 20 seconds (a letdown followed by a strong shot). This seems possible, but I also believe that one's shooting rhythm/speed is personal and only a small range of possibilities exists for any archer. (Why this is so I do not know and it is worth exploring scientifically, but what archer wants to forgo practicing what they think best to practice something else to answer such questions?)

So, maybe some can do this; if so, it is an option. The big question is: can it be done successfully?

Learning A Truncated Letdown Of all the options, this is the one I am currently favoring. This idea popped out of a drill called "Double Draws." In this drill, an archer draws to anchor, aims and then lets down to brace/pre-draw/set-up position, then draws again and finishes the shot. This is a conditioning drill but it might serve as a truncated letdown, too. According to my stopwatch a letdown takes as much time as a shot made in good order and can take longer if the letdown occurs because a shot is taking too long. This fact alone makes the use of an ordinary letdown on a 20-second shot perilous. But what if, when the letdown thought occurs (a sure trigger that you damn well better let down), one could drop to brace/pre-draw/set-up position and then continue? This would provide somewhat of a physical reset to accompany a mental reset program being run.

Doing the Double Draw drill provides physical conditioning benefits and can be a regular part of practice. Then some simulations under near-competitive conditions would inform the archer as to whether this would work to get past a letdown hang-up when on a 20-second shooting clock. If it does work, then the archer has this tool, a practiced tool, to bolster her confidence during competition.

Conclusion

If World Archery (FITA's new name) sticks with the 20 seconds per arrow rule for alternate shot competitions, it is clear we need to help archer-athletes cope with this problem. We have trained them to let down every time they need to let down, but that is not enough any more. I do not look forward, though, to training students to make the "least bad shot" they can rather than their best shot.

Additional Learning References
Shooting in the Now by Bob Ryder (AFm, Vol 17, No 1)
Shot Tempo Training by Van Webster (AFm, Vol 12, No 4)

Shooting Tips for Top Performance by Don Rabska (AFm, Vol 12, No 3)
Putting Your Form Under Pressure by Steve Ross (AFm, Vol 10, No 3)
Fatigue by Leighton Tau (AFm, Vol 9, No 6)
Controlling the Pace of Your Shot by Mike Gerard (AFm, Vol 4, No 4)
The 7 Habits of Successful Olympic Round Shooters by Lloyd Brown (AFm, Vol 2, No 5)

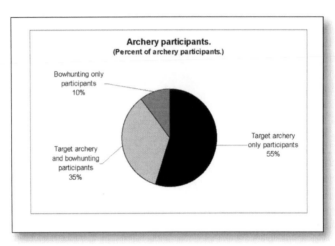

Archery participants.
(Percent of archery participants.)

Bowhunting only participants 10%

Target archery and bowhunting participants 35%

Target archery only participants 55%

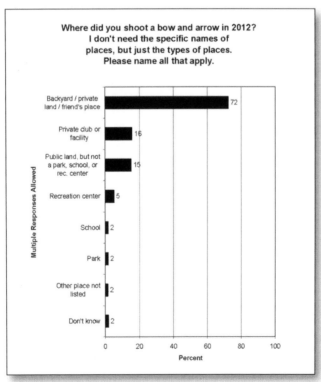

Where did you shoot a bow and arrow in 2012?
I don't need the specific names of
places, but just the types of places.
Please name all that apply.

Backyard / private land / friend's place — 72
Private club or facility — 16
Public land, but not a park, school, or rec. center — 15
Recreation center — 5
School — 2
Park — 2
Other place not listed — 2
Don't know — 2

Multiple Responses Allowed

Percent

Chapter 40
What Can We Learn from
ATA's Archery Participation Survey?

Previously I referred you to what in my knowledge is the first scientific study of participation in our sport. Here's the link again if you missed it—

www.archerytrade.org/uploads/documents/ATA_Participation_2013_Report_FINAL.pdf

Thanks to the Archery Trade Association for making the report public.

Prior Collective Wisdom

Before I get into comments about this study, here is my take on what the collective wisdom of archery folks was regarding the numbers of archers and bowhunters in this country. Estimates of the numbers of bowhunters were in the 3-3.5 million range. Estimates of target archers were even greater, primarily due to the large numbers of kids shooting arrows in summer camp (and that those kids notoriously didn't continue in the sport). The actual number of adult target archers was considered to be a very small fraction of the number of bowhunters. There are fewer than 50,000 registered members of the target archery associations and some of those are duplicates, as many of us belong to more than one such organization.

Archery manufacturers are focused primarily on bowhunters in this country as they believe there isn't much money to be made selling to target archers. Contrary to that stance, my personal assessment (an informal one) is that individual target archers buy more archery equipment and more expensive archery equipment than do bowhunters. Archery manufacturers don't sell clothing, deer stands, scents, food, cook stoves, calls, blinds, hunting licenses/permits, travel, lodging, etc. which makes up a great deal of the bowhunting market. Cabela's, by the way, makes most of its profits on . . . wait for it . . . clothing.

In support of the claim that the archery equipment of target archers tends to be higher end than that of bowhunters, consider how many X10s, Nano Pros, and the like are sold and what they cost compared to hunting shafts. About the only area of archery equipment that bowhunters outspend target archers is in arrow points. Target archers favor more expensive optics, bows, shafts, etc. You don't see many bowhunters buying computer programs and apps to determine their sight marks, nor do you see them buying $350 sights with $150 scopes or $300 release aids, for example. (Think about all of the handheld releases Carter Enterprises sells in target colors. Those aren't being sold for bowhunting.)

The Survey

Interestingly, the survey only counted adults. Of the kids (under 18) that participate in archery, I suspect that the vast majority are target archers only, but that is just a guess.

The survey firm conducted 8335 phone interviews, weighted according to all of the appropriate parameters. All surveyed were adults (in 2012, 23.5% of U.S. residents were under 18 years old and 76.5 were older, and since the population was 314 million people then, that works out to 240 million adults in 2012); 8% of all surveyed participated in archery (69% male, 31% female, and younger than the average adult, tending to be more rural than urban, more concentrated in the Midwest) which works out to, let's see 8% of 240 million adults is, 19 million archers in 2012 . . . not counting kids! Wow!

- 4.4% of the 8% were "target archery only" participants (55% of archers, 10.5 million)
- 0.8% of the 8% were "bowhunting only" participants (10% of archers, 1.92 million)
- 2.8% of the 8% were "target archery and bowhunting" participants (35% of archers, 6.7 million)

If my math is right, that means that 3.6% of those surveyed had a bowhunting archery experience in the survey year while 7.2% had a target archery experience.

Shockingly, there are more target archers than bowhunters!

With regard to equipment, 75% of those surveyed used compound bows (no surprise) but in response to the question "Where did you shoot a bow and arrow in 2012?"

- 72% said "back yard, private land, friends place" and
- 16% said "Private club or facility."

Another really telling question was: "What influenced you to become involved in archery?"

- 46% responded "A relative or family member"
- 17% said "A friend"

Other than "Scouts" all of the usual culprits (NASP, JOAD, camp, school, after school programs) accounted for 1% or less of the reasons people got involved. In fact, all of the "usual culprits" added up to a mere 7% of the total.

Comments

Clearly we need to a better job of marketing our sport in that all of our proactive efforts (fun shoots at county fairs and sporting gatherings, kids' programs, school programs, etc.) only account for 7% of the people in archery now (of course, that may be changing).

It also seems it is in the best interests of archery equipment manufacturers to promote target archery significantly more than they have in the past. If I am right, that a new target archer is worth more in sales than a new bowhunter, there are significant amounts of money to be made selling to target archers.

A little research on the Internet showed that 11 million kids every summer attend summer camps (American Camp Association/ACA estimate). I didn't pay for access to the ACA's data report but they have published the fact that "over half of their camps are "resident" camps and that in those camps, archery was the third most popular activity." So, as a rough estimate, I would say that 4-6 million kids experience archery in camps every year. I also happen to know that archery youth groups don't have populations anywhere near that big so I suspect that one of the biggest problems is program accessibility. If every one of those kids who got jazzed on archery at summer camp and on their way home drove right by a convenient archery facility, I can't imagine that they would not be clamoring to "check it out." My experience is that our archery clubs and ranges might as well be camouflaged, they are so well hidden.

What do you think?

Additional Learning References

Helping Them Buy Their Own Archery Gear by AER (AFm, Vol 14, No 5)
Golf Envy by Steve Ruis (AFm, Vol 10, No 6)
Archery Beyond 55 by Dean Pridgen (AFm, Vol 9, No 3)
Tips on Running More Enjoyable and More Profitable Archery Leagues
by Tom Dorigatti (AFm, Vol 8, No 6)
Designing an Archery Course by Van Webster (AFm, Vol 8, No 6)
Starting an Archery Program from Scratch by Steve Ruis (AFm, Vol 8, No 5)
Fundraising Fun! by Mike Gerard (AFm, Vol 5, No 5)
Finding New Members—One Club's Search by Kerry Jaeger (AFm, Vol 4, No 5)

At our club in California a competitor in our annual fundraising novelty shoot got banned indefinitely from our range for tearing the antlers off of one of the targets in a rage (not this one).
Bad behavior can be destructive as well as offensive.

Chapter 41
There Must Be a Better Way

This is an unusual subject in that I am addressing only those of you who want to achieve the very highest goals. This came about because of a comment made by my partner, Claudia. She enjoys reading biographies of high-performing individuals and she is often struck by the fact that these high performers tend to be, well, not very nice people.

In discussing this with her I thought, well maybe if you weren't a "bad boy," people wouldn't be interested in your biography and while that might be in part true, it certainly isn't the whole situation. (Many of these outrageous high performers were dead before their books came out.)

I then thought of the NFL and the large number of players who, having just done something really well, run off away from their teammates to bask in their moment of glory. Often they do this when their team is losing badly and it seems really inappropriate. Certainly such behaviors don't build team cohesion. The act of separating oneself from the group because you did something particularly well is done in the theatre, but only at the urging of the other actors. (Go ahead, take another bow; you earned it!) Try that without such gestures and expect to be snubbed back stage. And then there is the high concentration of criminals in the NFL. Many of those football players are not nice people at all. (Read the book "Pros and Cons: The Criminals Who Play in the NFL" by Jeff Benedict and Don Yaeger if you doubt this.) Apologists might claim that football is a violent sport, so it attracts violent people, and I would guess there is some truth to that, but it also seems that egotistical behavior and high achievement go very much hand in hand.

I don't mean to invoke Charlie Sheen frivolously, but there are plenty of examples of bad behavior from the acting profession as well. It is not just sports.

Is Archery Immune to Bad Behavior?
Archery is such a genteel sport; certainly such bad behavior isn't seen in our ranks? Suggest that to anyone with a couple of decades in archery and you will elicit any number of stories disabusing you of such a thought. Archery is not immune. I don't mean to say that bad behaviors are rampant, as I do not think they are, but my primary concern right now is . . . you.

Archers have been known to stamp off, retiring from a competition without telling anyone, just getting in their cars and leaving. Archers have been known to swing their bows at trees as if they were baseball bats. Archers have been known to destroy targets in fits of anger. Archers have been known to intimidate (or try to intimidate) other archers. Archers have been known to abuse organizers of events by withholding their participation from ceremonies. Archers . . . well, you get the idea.

There are enough other stories available of archers feeling lost and alone, even depressed, from only taking a silver medal in the Olympics (after all, they had failed!). There are even stories of athletes becoming depressed after having won. These situations are not unexpected because achieving at a very high level seems to require a great deal of single mindedness, to the point where one's behavior becomes obsessive.

This does not have to be the only way to victory. Let's look at what we can do as archers and coaches to minimize bad behavior and maximize our satisfaction.

An Athlete's Role

No matter how much importance has been loaded into a particular tournament or series of tournaments, your role is to enjoy the process, because what does it all matter if you win and your friends, teammates, and family are embarrassed to talk about it or you?

It is time for now famous (infamous?) "it's the journey, not the destination" trope to get trotted out, a phrase so many self-help sources tout. And there is a core of truth in it. The existence of "happy warrior" athletes shows us winning need not be arduous or a travail.

I subscribe to the axiom: "There must be joy." Think about what "en•joy•ment" means. If you take no joy from practice or competition, why are you doing it? A great many of the athletic "heroes" of my youth were perpetually mad, which I would find a complete misery. But they were highly paid for their work and their anger was a source of energy that fueled their performances. I even use this source myself. I discovered this when I made a poor first shot in a club championship shootoff. I got really mad about that shot, mad at myself, and I used that "mad" to focus in and win that shootoff. If I used that technique every time I shot, I would be an emotional wreck in no time, though.

When I say "there must be joy" I am not talking about being giddy with laughter. I am talking about the deep satisfaction I find in performing well in practice or in competition. Win or lose, if I compete well, I find joy in the competition. Archery is a sport, like golf, that has no defense. You can't prevent somebody from shooting a better score than you. You just have to acknowledge that on that day, they mastered the range better than you did.

Pick Your Models As a recommendation I suggest that you don't just study the technical skills of the archers you admire but study those who win with class and kindness and generosity. If your archery model is a jerk, then maybe you are getting the wrong message.

Being Other-Directed vs. Being Self-Directed As an archer, ask yourself: "If you shot a perfect FITA Round (or NFAA Field Round, or any other really challenging round) in practice, a feat never before done, would you be exultant, even if no one else saw it?" Do you need an audience or are you competing for yourself?

Some people are quite self-contained and they need very little emotional or other support from other people. We say these people are "self-directed." Others require the people around them to give them feedback as to how they stand. These are not necessarily "needy" people, they just need a little help from their friends. We call these folks "other-directed." Think about which of these two types you are closest to. That knowledge will help you determine how you need to behave. In order to get reliable feedback from people, you need to know them well enough to be able to evaluate whether their advice is based upon knowing you well and knowing archery well or not. If you need a lot of feedback, you need to develop a lot of "archery friends" who you can count on. If you do not, well, we do not suggest you are free to abuse the people around you. Sometimes you are dependent upon the kindness of strangers. (Can you call this arrow for me?) In general we recommend at the minimum a "professional" deportment, if not outright being accepting and supportive of those around you.

A Coach's Role

Coaches can help to shape their archer-athlete's attitudes. On this path, we have helped archers by staging rehearsal medal ceremonies, so they would know what to do in that event. We also ask our students to have goals going into competitions. For our relatively new archers we ask that one performance goal and one deportment goal be written ahead of time and discussed afterward. The performance goal is a process goal, not an outcome goal. "I will win a medal" is an outcome goal. "I will use my mental program on every shot" is a process goal. Outcome goals are focused on what you want to achieve; process goals are focused on how you think you can achieve a better performance (leading to desired outcomes, of course). Obviously process goals are more important for archers on steep learning curves. For first competitions we recommend that "to have fun" is a great first process goal. In effect, this is a recommendation to enjoy the process.

Deportment goals are goals based on your behavior, things like "I will not trash talk during the event." We hope that this creates in our athlete's minds that there is more than a competition going on. Reputations are being created; relationships, too. If you put off somebody who would make a great shooting partner, you lose.

Coaching Bad Boys Ask any sports fan if they have ever seen a coach "go ballistic" on an athlete. Essentially all will say "yes." Unfortunately too may will mention youth sports right away (my first such was in Little League). College coaches behaving this way is far too common. Poor behavior on the part of coaches should be looked on with even more opprobrium than that of archers. Archers are at least in the heat of competition or working desperately to improve. Coaches are one or more steps removed from that process and should emotionally be one or more steps removed, too. Coaches who get really upset at athletes at practices or tournaments have to reconsider whether it is about them or their archers.

Conclusion

If we want to have a wholesome, supportive sport, then archers and coaches are obligated to consider their own behaviors and how they present our sport to onlookers, be they other archers or spectators.

Additional Learning References

Do Not Let Fear Affect Your Archery by Stan Popovitch (AFm, Vol 15, No 5)
Preparing for Pressure by Troy Bassham (AFm, Vol 13, No 5)
Take a Deep Breath by Alison Rhodius (AFm, Vol 12, No 6)
Control by Alistair Whittingham (AFm, Vol 12, No 3)
Dealing With Distractions, Pt 1 & 2 by Lanny Bassham (AFm, Vol 12, No 3 & 4)
Competition—The Good, The Bad, and the Ugly by James A. Swan, Ph.D. (AFm, Vol 9, No 4)
Coaching With Kindness by Lisa Franseen, Ph.D. (AFm, Vol 5, No 2)
Coaching Your Child—Without Losing Your Child by Lyle Stratton (AFm, Vol 4, No 3)

Ever have to convince anyone of the safety and benefits of an archery instructional program, like a parks and recreation board? It can be daunting.

Chapter 42
The Benefits of Archery

Coaches are often put into the position of having to sell our sport to some extent. Most parents just see their kids having fun doing it and are satisfied. Others want a bit more. They want to know if it is safe. They want to know if there are other benefits beyond just "it's fun."

Also, if you are an entrepreneurial coach, you may be in the position of having to convince a Park Director or a Parks and Rec Board of the merits of having an archery class. So what do you say?

Here is something I wrote for this purpose. I hope it helps. (It was written for a "lay" audience, that is, for non-archers.)

The Benefits of Archery

Archery is a wonderful sport for kids, primarily because it doesn't select out certain body types. You don't have to be tall, as for basketball, or fast as for track, or big as for football, or strong, or particularly well-coordinated, or. . . . What archery requires from its participants is the ability to relax and focus while under the tension of the drawn bow. Consequently, archery is the sport for kids who aren't attracted to other sports or who aren't particularly athletic.

An especially nice aspect of archery is that, if an archer struggles with a pulling force of a bow (called the "draw weight") they can be given another bow, one they can pull comfortably. There are no set equipment sizes (like the size of a baseball, softball, or shot put), per se. So, the equipment can always be made to "fit" the archer. Relaxing and focusing on what you are doing while under tension: this is required for good archery and is the source of the core benefits. Archery clears the mind and refreshes the body. There can be considerable walking, fresh air, and sunshine involved, too.

Also, because of safety considerations, archers learn appreciation for their own safety and the safety of others. This is a lesson in being responsible and also in interacting with others who might not be being responsible. Archery is a social sport and a great deal of self-correcting goes on within the body of archers. As is sadly true in other sports, some archers insist on breaking, or trying to break, the rules of safety or competition. Since archery is largely self-regulating, people have to learn to have good boundaries and how to address a difficult situation with tact and effectiveness. In this, archery is a microcosm of life. Golf has a wonderful tradition that golfers are expected to call rule violations upon themselves; archery is not quite there yet. Don't get me wrong, the vast majority of archers practice and compete without trying to get an unfair advantage. But in cases where some do, one has to deal with them forthrightly.

Archers learn self-discipline. To have one arrow go into the center of the target is very nice but to have all of the arrows go there requires that shot after shot be made the same way. One must school one's body and one's mind to achieve repeatable accuracy.

Archery is an individual sport; there is no one else to blame if things go poorly. But archery goes on to teach archers that blame is counterproductive. If one shoots a bad arrow, one must accept it and go on to the next. If one doesn't do that, the upset surrounding the blaming will cause arrow after arrow to be shot poorly. Archery teaches acceptance of the things that one cannot change (the last shot) and commitment to things one can change (the next shot).

There is also an aspect of archery that promotes civility and self-reliance—there is no defense in archery. You cannot prevent someone from besting your score and winning a competition; you can only depend upon yourself. Trying to affect another archer negatively so as to increase your chance of winning is bad sportsmanship and will be corrected by instructors and other archers.

We cannot tell you what your child will get from archery but we can tell you what parents of our participants tell us and what studies show. Parents tell us:

- *"It is the only thing that gets him away from his video games!"*
- *"She loves archery and willingly does her chores to make sure she can come to class each week."*
- *"My son is overweight and not a great student. But he is actually very good at archery. I think having something he can be proud of makes a big difference."*
- *"It broke my heart to see my daughter give up dance when her body changed; she felt she could never excel without the typical dancer's physique. Now she's excelling at archery, and she tells me she's going to the Olympics and I believe her."*
- *"My son is—how do you say this?—a negotiator. With archery the safety rules are non-negotiable, the score on the target is non-negotiable, and there's nobody to argue with. He would go to archery class every day if he could."*
- *"My son has ADHD and archery has been amazing for him. He only has to focus for a short time, during the actual shot, then he can relax, and then focus again. He's self-motivated with archery and I love the way his coach lets him proceed at his own pace."*
- *"We actually shoot as a family. It's difficult to find something that we all want to do together, and archery night at the rec center is it. We compete for who has to do the dishes."*
- *(In response to a question as to whether the fees were appropriate)* *"Are you kidding? I spent $260 on a just pair of skates when my kid was doing ice hockey!"*
- *"It's just nice to have something that she's passionate about, and for some reason it's archery. I don't really get it, but since it makes her happy, I'm happy."*

In addition, studies of the participants in the National Archery in the Schools Program show that school kids have higher attendance and more attentiveness when archery is in session in P.E. Some teachers have made participation in archery dependent on turning in homework and other school activities and have seen positive responses.

Archery is Safe

Archery is one of the safest of recreational activities, primarily because safety is woven into the fabric of the sport. This is at least mildly surprising in that archery is a form of weapons training. Beginners in archery are taught safety from the first lesson onward. These lessons are reinforced until they become habits.

When you sign your child up for an introductory archery class, there are certain things you can look for as signs that the program is a safe one. For one, parents should be welcome to observe – with limitations.

Parental Involvement In our programs the limitations on parental involvement are simple: we do not want parents exhorting or coaching their child while we are working with them. The reason is this: their voice cuts through all of the other voices out there. If I am trying to make a point with your child and a parent's voice breaks her attention (as it should), she may miss something important that might turn out to be dangerous to her or to other students. When your child is done at the shooting line and comes back from it, parents are welcome to talk all they want, but we ask them to please not talk through what the coach is trying to say, even if you are encouraging your child to listen to the coach!

We have always wanted parents to be involved. The most important reason is safety. The only significant accident we have had over the years involved a student-archer who was behind the shooting line within arm's reach of two instructors. All extra pairs of eyes are valuable. This is especially true if your child is receiving instruction on a field range. In this case, archers follow a winding trail from target to target in a manner similar to the holes on a golf course. Because of this aspect, all of the equipment (bows, arrows, etc.) must be carried along the path. Since the trail is narrow, it is often the case that not all of the student-archers can shoot at one time. So some will shoot while others wait several feet behind the shooting position. While the instructor's focus is on the archers shooting arrows, the others may try to get into mischief. Parent's can monitor the behavior of those waiting while the instructor is busy.

Safety Behaviors You should see a number of safety behaviors both built into your child's program and being taught to participating kids. A simple one is that, for beginners, the triad of child–bow–arrows only comes together on the shooting line. Often this is done by leaving the arrows at the shooting line (sometimes bows, too). Children walking around with both bow and arrows shouldn't happen until a considerable amount of instruction has occurred, even on field ranges. When young student-archers have graduated from leaving the arrows at the shooting line in a "ground quiver" to wearing a "belt quiver" to carry their arrows, they will be trained that the only time an arrow can be taken out of their quiver is when they are in their shooting position on a designated shooting line.

Another safety behavior that needs constant reinforcement is that "We always walk on the archery range!" Excited archers wanting to observe their first bull's-eye are tempted to run to the target. This is not allowed because runners can trip, and if they do trip they can fall into a target bristling with sharp arrows. (Yes, the back ends of arrows—the nock ends—are sharp enough to cause a puncture wound.) In a good program you should not see children running around, with or without archery equipment in hand, as a running child can crash into another.

Note that "archery range rules" are typically stated as what "can be done" rather than what "cannot be done." This is purposeful as the list of things that cannot be done is very, very long. Even stating some of those forbidden things can put thoughts in young minds that might not have occurred to them. A rule that was in vogue in the past was "Do not shoot arrows straight up in the air." This rule has now been replaced by the rule "We only shoot at the targets." The idea of shooting straight up in the air might never have occurred to a child and that rule doesn't cover such options as: shooting over the road next to the range, shooting at trees, shooting at animals passing through the range, shooting into the pond, trying to shoot a fish in the pond, shooting rocks, etc. I think you get the idea. Archery range rules are simple and should specify what can be done, not what cannot be done. Also, it is best that these rules be posted; that way the instructor can tell kids that he or she is just "enforcing the range rules" and not having to spend personal authority to do so.

Archery instructors should exhibit "zero tolerance" for violations of the safety rules; each violation needs to be corrected. We often address the whole group when an individual violates a safety rule, as it is a "teaching moment" and this prevents embarrassment to the rule violator. First violations receive a verbal correction. If the same rule is violated after a correction, that child will typically have to sit out one cycle of shooting (one "end" of shooting) as punishment. A child who willfully or mischievously violates a rule will be asked to sit out the rest of the session (or be sent home if a parent is there). Repeat violators are removed from the class. This is a progressive discipline system that should be applied rigorously and fairly to all children. An instructor who overlooks safety violations or who "plays favorites" is a bad sign—this is not a good program.

By the time your child reaches an intermediate level, there are almost no safety violations because all of the safety behaviors are habit at that point. (We move on to fun topics like, "Why you shouldn't 'talk trash' during a competition.")

Whistling Along In target archery groups our archers are given directions using a whistle. This system is used in youth classes all of the way to world championships and the Olympic Games (they use a horn instead of a whistle, but the system is the same).

Here is the system:

The Whistle System

Two Blasts	Archers may come to the shooting line
One Blast	Archers may place an arrow on the bow and begin shooting
Three Blasts	Archers may walk to the target to retrieve their arrows
Five or More Blasts	Emergency! Stop immediately and wait for instructions

This system is safe because the instructors control the whistle. They only give the "two blasts" if everyone is behind the waiting line and is behaving correctly. They only give the "one blast" if everyone on the shooting line has taken a stance (with one foot on either side of the line) and everyone else is behind the waiting line and is behaving correctly. If anyone reaches for an arrow before the one blast, they will be corrected and the "one whistle" signal will not be given until all arrows are back in the quivers.

When everyone has shot their arrows and retired to the waiting line, the instructor either blows two more blasts (for a second group/line of archers) or three blasts to allow archers to retrieve their arrows.

This system works because if anyone acts up, no one gets to shoot. This builds peer pressure on those inclined to not follow the rules. Similarly, if someone begins to run to their target, the emergency whistle blasts stop everyone in their tracks, while that person gets corrected.

Your participants should be taught this system within the first couple of classes

Training young archers to be safe as a matter of habit is why the sport has such a sterling safety record. If you want further information on the safety of archery, take a look at this report http://nasparchery.com/data/nasparchery/file/321_5541_ArcherySafetyInsight.pdf.

Safety doesn't stop with the archery-specific aspects. Children out in the sun for long periods still need sunscreen, hydrating fluids, etc.

Conclusion
You are welcome to present this to anyone interested in the benefits of archery. You can tell them I wrote it or you can tell them you wrote it, I don't care, as long as people see the benefits of our wonderful sport and support places where it can be practiced.

Additional Learning References
A Parent's Guide to Archery by Steve Ruis (AFm, Vol 13, No 5) Sadly, this is the only book available for archery parents. There should be more. Covers most of the basics.
SafeSport Certification by Van Webster (AFm, Vol 17, No 6)
Just How Important is Safety? by Steve Ruis (AFm, Vol 16, No 4)
Kids and Archery by Kevin Foss (AFm, Vol 14, No 3)
Kids and Archery Classes by Van Webster (AFm, Vol 11, No 1)
Got Archery? by Tim Scronce (AFm, Vol 9, No 3)
Archery is Fun for the Whole Family by Ava McDowell (AFm, Vol 8, No 5)

Pulling and carrying arrows has to be taught, einforced, and monitored in order to establish safe habits for archers.

Still More on Coaching Archery

Chapter 43
Having a Lot of Pull
on the Archery Range

I was a Judge at a rather successful JOAD tournament yesterday and one of the things that made it successful was the inclusion of "novices." These were archers who had had only a couple of lessons. The target faces were big, the distances short, and the number of arrows shot reduced. "But, but, that is not an official round!" you say. True, but, who cares? Each of the novices was given a small participation medal and got to see the medals won by the kids shooting in class. (There was also a slew of parents there to watch!).

The tournament organizer told me that all of the brand new archers who had shot as a "novice" the previous summer in a similar event, shot in an official JOAD class in the state indoor championships that winter. (All of them, every last one of them.) So, I ask you, do you think that was worth doing?

One of the things I saw that the novices and the "seasoned" JOAD competitors had in common was the inability to pull arrows correctly. I saw every recommended safe practice violated numerous times by archers in both groups. Since this event was put on as a rehearsal event for the state outdoor championships three weeks away, this was an opportunity to educate these young archers, so we did.

Here's a review of why we do things the way we do when pulling arrows.

Having a Lot of Pull on the Archery Range: The Principles
There are some basic principles are involved:

Safety, Safety, Safety The second most common injury in archery is getting poked (or stabbed) by the nock end of an arrow being pulled. When arrows are being pulled, the pullers and the archers/scorers watching need to be to either side. We tell our young archers that the area right in front of the target is the Danger Zone and that the Danger Zone extends back at least their full arm span from the nocks of the arrows.

We Are Building Habits (Safe Habits) By insisting on arrows being pulled a certain way, we are building habits that will serve these archers well later on. Everything that can be relegated to the realm of habit is something they don't have to think about. Those activities become things that they "always do that way." This means they have fewer distractions and concerns when competing and, of course, will be safer.

Habits are Built Through Repetition So Reinforcement is Needed Coaches need to monitor arrow pulling and reinforce the correct ways to do things. You have to do this over and over and over for each group of newbies you work with. This is not the most fun part of coaching youth archery, but you knew the job was dangerous when you took it, no? If you don't insist on it being done the right way, they will form a habit anyway—a habit of doing it the wrong way. So help them make habits that serve them well: tell them over and over how to do it the right way (and why, if they ask).

Having a Lot of Pull on the Archery Range: The Procedures

The procedures are how we do the task. Why we do it the way we do, coaches need to know. Archers don't necessarily need to know "why," but some are curious and it doesn't hurt to explain.

Archers Must Always Respect the Danger Zone Before pulling an arrow, we teach our archers to look over their shoulder to check that the Danger Zone is clear. We instruct the archers waiting to pull to not only vacate the Danger Zone but to check that no other archers are in the Danger Zone before pulling starts. This creates a situation in which at least two people are responsible for checking the Danger Zone before pulling starts.

Pull Arrows with an Empty Hand I saw a great many pullers pulling arrows while holding other arrows in their hand. This is a good way to crack, bend, or dent arrow shafts while pulling. If this becomes a habit, this will happen sooner or later. In addition, if there is something already in their pulling hand, they are more likely to slip while pulling. The pulling hand must be empty when an arrow is pulled. So, our rule is "Pull One, Quiver One." If the archers haven't graduated to a worn quiver yet, we teach them to "Pull One, Drop One." Yes, on the ground or floor. After all of the arrows are pulled, they pick theirs up and make a bundle to carry back.

Loose Arrows are Carried in One Hand There seems to be a disagreement amongst coaches as to how archers are to carry loose arrows. There should not be. There is one and only one safe way to do this. Here it is: the arrows are bundled together all pointing the same way. The group is tamped on the ground or target butt so all of the arrow points are side-by-side. The arrows are then carried with one hand wrapped around those points.

The bouquet of arrows can have their fletches point up or down, it doesn't matter. The archers only needs to know that if they are bumped or tripped that they are to hold onto the arrows for dear life. If they do that, they cannot be injured by those arrows except in an almost trivial way. The reason for this is the angle of the wrist. There is no way that an archer can accidentally or deliberately poke himself in the face with the nock ends of those arrows. (Try it. Take a bundle of long arrows, points in hand and try to point the nocks at your face.) The arrows are too long for their wrists to bend far enough to point them back it their head. The only possible injury from the arrows is the nock ends might impact the archer's feet or ankles. That's it.

If the archers, as some recommend, carry the arrows with two hands, there is an immediate problem. If they get bumped or trip, when they fall to the ground, they do not consciously decide which hand or arm will be disengaged from holding the arrows to break their fall. Since only one hand can be wrapped around the arrow points, if that hand gets released in an effort to break the fall, a great many nasty scenarios become possible including falling upon the arrows with the points facing the archer.

Loose arrows are bundled and carried in one hand, with that hand wrapped around the arrow points. Period.

Your Feet Don't Move Until the Arrows are Secure If your archers are walking back to the target sorting or quivering their arrows an accident can occur (tripping, spooked by a squirrel running under foot, you name it) with arrows in dangerous configurations. So, teach your student-archers to secure all of their arrows before taking their first step in walking back to the shooting line. The first step is critical because, well, one thing leads to another.

When Pulling: Don't Twist Many beginning archers twist their arrows thinking that this will help remove them. While this might work for arrows that are barely penetrating the butt, it is a recipe for cracked or broken or bent arrows that are in deeper. Teach them to pull without twisting. If they are struggling to remove an arrow, get them into the habit of asking another archer to pull with them. The first archer grasps the arrow with their hand against the target butt, the second archer grasps it right behind and they both pull. If the second archer grasps farther back, the arrow shaft may get bent (if aluminum) or cracked (if carbon), so that is to be discouraged.

When Pulling: Don't Reach At this shoot, I watched one young archer pull her arrow that was closest to her and then reached for the next and then for the next until she was at almost a 45 degree angle to the ground. Maybe she was focused on her arrows so intently that she didn't think to keep her feet under her. I saw other archers trying to pull arrows high on the target butt on tiptoes. In order to be safe archers have to pull from strong body positions: feet on the ground underneath them, one hand to push against the butt, the pulling hand on top of the arrow and up against the butt, and preferable using their dominant arm to pull. If they are on the wrong side of the target butt to use their dominant arm, they must not use their dominant arm back-handed because that is a weak position. If they can't pull an arrow with their non-dominant arm, they should wait until they can get at it from the other side of the target. Also, tall archers are used to being asked to help pull arrows high in the target butt, so have your students learn to ask them.

Similarly if they begin pulling their arrows and then find a whole bunch of other arrows in the way, they should not reach for them, through or around those arrows. Instead they should step back and wait until those arrows are pulled and then address their remaining arrows with the others out of the way.

Conclusion

Obviously there are a lot of things to be learned here and some of them are nuanced, so you can't expect new archers to learn them immediately, especially if you believe as we do that archers learn best by doing. This means coaches need to reinforce all aspects of pulling arrows as part of safety instruction, which, of course, has our highest priority.

Creating safe habits while on the archery range should be our number one goal when we work with beginners. We want them to have fun, like our sport, and continue to participate, and getting injured is no fun at all.

Additional Learning References

Just How Important is Safety? by Steve Ruis (AFm, Vol 16, No 4)
A Parent's Guide to Archery by Steve Ruis
Finding Arrows in the Grass by Steve Ruis (AFm, Vol 12, No 5)

Uh, let's see . . . breathing . . . it goes from here . . . to about here.
(Photo Courtesy of Andy Macdonald)

Still More on Coaching Archery

Chapter 44
Random Archery Thoughts

These are a bunch of tidbits that individually didn't make for whole chapters. They are all related to archery but originated from other sports.

Where Are We Going?

According to one school of thought, we go through four stages when learning complex processes. They are:

UI (Unconscious Incompetence)

CI (Conscious Incompetence)

CC (Conscious Competence)

UC (Unconscious Competence)

We all start at UI, unconscious incompetence, that is we don't know what to do either consciously or subconsciously. All we can see is that we are doing whatever it is wrong and we are unaware of what is wrong and how to make it right.

The next stage is that we become aware of our incompetence, CI or conscious incompetence. This is exemplified by the youth, typically male, who insists they know how to do everything (as they have seen it done maybe, yet find themselves unable to do it when presented by the opportunity).

With practice we can reach the next stage, CC or conscious competence, where we can do the thing but only by concentrating and thinking through the process in a fairly clumsy way. Finally we reach the desired state, UC or unconscious competence, in which we can do the task as if on autopilot.

We have all been through these stages countless times. Think about learning to tie your own shoes or learning to drive a car. When we were young our parents or an older sibling tied our shoes for us. At some point we began to get instruction in this oh-so-vital task. Initially we were very confused and couldn't remember what to do (UI), then we became aware how complex this damned thing was and knew we would never learn this (CI), but with persistence and with someone talking us through it we got to the point we could talk ourselves through it (CC) and then, after much more practice we got to where we are today, UC. Today, you tie your shoes without a conscious thought or concern.

Think about these stages with regard to when you learned to drive. You will recognize the same points. They apply to archers, too. Practice is where we build CC on the path to becoming UC. This is where the maxim "practice consciously, perform subconsciously" come from.

The Care and Feeding of Our Subconscious Minds

Scientists are just beginning to map out unconscious mental processes through the creative use by researchers of brain scanners. While a great deal has been written about our "subconscious" minds and processes, the best we could characterize them was as "capabilities that we don't have to think about." Until we get better science, we are stuck with groping in the dark for answers when it comes to subconscious processes. A comment from a golfer brought this to mind. He said: "Our subconscious believes everything we tell it, so I've learned to laugh at bad shots."

Obviously you are not trying to train your subconscious brain to consider bad shots (golf or archery) as a source of humor. You are just trying to not make them overwhelmingly negative. You do not want any kind of very emotional response to any shot. You want to be able to coolly analyze the bad shot to figure out how to make sure the next one is a good one.

In golf, you virtually never hit the same shot twice (except those damned uphill chip shots that roll back down the slope you were trying to get them up). In archery it is typical that the next shot is exactly like the previous one. And if you imprinted on the bad shot, you just made it easier to repeat. Getting really angry is a way to imprint something, so it is preferable that you minimize the emotional impact. Mix a little "positive" reaction with the automatic negative reaction you will get anyway, figure out what you did wrong and get the next one right.

Breathe! Sure, but When?

The question is: 'Should you breathe out or in when drawing the bow?" I have mentioned elsewhere that weight lifters breathe out when lifting. Studies show that this keeps blood pressures down and blood flows up, so it is an advantage. A guy on the Internet mentioned that he was taught the opposite in a clinic he took on high-performance tennis. The clinic leaders showed the validity of this by having them try to clench their fists while breathing out and while holding their breath. They found it way more difficult to clench their fists as they exhaled, but they could do it easily when they inhaled or held their breath. Since they don't want to tense their muscles, they were told that they shouldn't hold their breath. They said that if you watch a tennis player losing his smoothness, he is probably holding his breath. Cheeks puffed out is the sign.

So, which is it? Breathe in or breathe out (or hold it) while drawing?

I think this is fairly easy to settle. Weight lifters are exerting much greater forces than tennis players or archers. With much less force involved, I don't think whether you breath in or out is as critical as it is for lifters. Also, tennis players have to be loose and flexible while running about swinging their racquets because they need to be quick to respond to fast moving tennis balls. Archers do not need to do this, but we also don't find unnecessary muscle tension to be a help either.

So, I suggest you work backward from where you need to be at full draw just before the string is loosed. Studies have been alluded to that we are steadiest when we are holding somewhat less than a full breath. So, at full draw we want to be holding our breath, but not a quite full one. So, having taken a full breath, we let a little out and voila, we are ready to loose. This corresponds to breathing in on the draw.

Or does it?

I have asthma and I shoot mostly a compound bow. Compound archers typically spend more time at full draw than do recurve/longbow archers. If I follow the breath in while drawing recommendation, I frequently run out of gas at full draw. So, I breathe out during the draw, then breath in while I am settling into the shot, finding my anchor, lining up peep and scope and checking the leveling bubble, then I breath out a bit and finish the shot.

I hope this has convinced you that there is no one "right" breathing pattern for archers and that it is something that you need to address to make your shot complete and working for you.

Additional Learning References

Take a Deep Breath by Alison Rhodius (AFm, Vol 12, No 6)
Remember to Breathe by Leighton Tyau (AFm, Vol 9, No 5)
Conscious vs. Unconscious Aiming by Rick McKinney (AFm, Vol 6, No 2)

About the Author

Steve Ruis is an avid archer and coach. He has a Level 4 Coaching Certificate from USA Archery and a Master Coach certificate from the National Field Archery Association and recently became certified by U.S. Collegiate Archery. Since 1999, he has been the editor of *Archery Focus* magazine which is distributed worldwide and was at one point being translated into Italian, French, German, and Spanish. He has written numerous articles about archery and coaching for that magazine and for others. He has medalled in national- and state-level competitions but his proudest archery accomplishment is being a three-time club champion of the Nevada County Sportsmens Club (Nevada City, CA). He is co-author/editor of *Precision Archery* (with Claudia Stevenson) which has sold over 16,000 copies. More recently he has written *Coaching Archery, More on Coaching Archery, Archery for Kids,* and *A Parent's Guide to Archery, Winning Archery, Why You Suck at Archery, Shooting Arrows (Archery for Adult Beginners),* and *Archery Coaching How To's.*

The Watching Arrows Fly Catalog

The Watching Arrows Fly Coaching Library

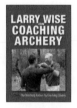 **Larry Wise on Coaching Archery** (2014)
by Larry Wise
For compound and
bowhunting coaches.

Archery Coaching How To's (2013)
by Steve Ruis
For those coaching out of their area of
experise and beginning-to-intermediate
coaches.

 **Even More on Coaching Archery** (2013)
by Steve Ruis
Even more coaching advice for all coaches.

More on Coaching Archery (2010)
by Steve Ruis
More coaching advice for all coaches.

 **Coaching Archery** (2008)
by Steve Ruis
For beginning-to-intermediate
coaches.

All Titles Available on Amazon.com

General Archery Titles

ProActive Archery (2012)
by Tom Dorigatti
For compound archers wanting to be really good.

Professional Archery Technique (2009)
by Kirk Ethridge
Third Edition
Primarily for compound and 3-D archers.

Why You Suck at Archery (2012)
by Steve Ruis
Written for archers who want to learn why they aren't getting better and how they can.

Winning Archery (2012)
by Steve Ruis
You learned how to shoot, now learn how to win .

Shooting Arrows (2012)
by Steve Ruis
Written to help adults cope with their new sport.

Confessions of an Archery Mom (2011)
by Lorretta Sinclair
Stories of an Archery Mom coping with three boys, all outstanding archers.

Archery 4 Kids (2010)
by Steve Ruis
Written for 8 to 14-year old beginners.

A Parent's Guide to Archery (2010)
by Steve Ruis
Written to help parents who have children in archery.

ArcheryFocus
m a g a z i n e

Has What You Need to Know to Become a Better Archer or Coach

Available OnLine at
www.archeryfocus.com

There are lots of books about archery—about archery form, archery execution, archery equipment, even archery history; but there weren't any books in print on archery coaching . . . until now. Finally there is a book on coaching for beginning to intermediate archery coaches. In **Coaching Archery** you will learn not *what* to teach (which you can get that from those other books) but *how* to teach it and much more you won't get from certification courses. Topics include:

- tips on running programs
- the styles of archery
- the mental side of archery
- an exploration of archery coaching styles
- helping with equipment
- coaching at tournaments
- plus, advice on becoming a better coach from some top coaches

There are even seven whole pages of resources for coaches! If you are a archery coach looking to increase your coaching skills, this is the book for you!

128 pages • ISBN 978-0-9821471-0-8 • US $19.95

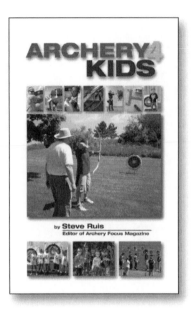

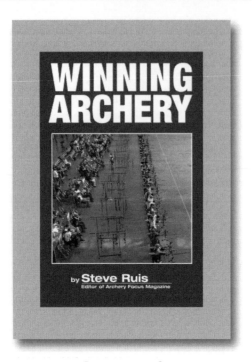

Notes

Notes

Printed in Great Britain
by Amazon.co.uk, Ltd.,
Marston Gate.